An Introduction to the Social and Economic History of Germany

An Introduction to the Social and Economic History of Germany

Politics and Economic Change in the Nineteenth and Twentieth Centuries

HELMUT BÖHME

Translated with an editorial introduction by W. R. Lee

BASIL BLACKWELL / OXFORD

Originally published as
*Prolegomena zu einer Sozial- und
Wirtschaftsgeschichte Deutschlands*
© Suhrkamp Verlag 1972
and translated by arrangement

British Library Cataloguing in Publication Data

Böhme, Helmut
  An introduction to the social and economic history
  of Germany.
  1. Germany – Social conditions
  I. Title II. Lee, W R
  309.1'43   HN445

  ISBN 0–631–17570–9

Phototypeset in V.I.P. Melior by
Western Printing Services Ltd, Bristol.
Printed and bound in Great Britain
by Billing and Son Ltd.,
London, Guildford and Worcester.

Contents

Editor's Introduction

The crisis of historicism has been voiced on innumerable occasions. History, it has been claimed, 'fails to fulfil its social function – in government, in administration, in all the manifold affairs of men'[1]*. In a society increasingly orientated according to the criterion of social utility, the absence of a recognisable and accepted social function could indeed be viewed as a severe, if not insuperable, hindrance for any academic discipline. The position of the discipline and in particular what is known as 'Fachhistorie' in Germany would, however, seem to be even more precarious than in the United Kingdom. The latent dilemma of historicism was pinpointed after the First World War, when Heuss referred to the need to reappraise Nietzsche's original questioning of the usefulness of history as a whole as far as the practical problems of life were concerned.[2] The historian Fritz Stern,[3] while stressing that the tensions between history and the social sciences were a common phenomenon in the western world, nevertheless viewed this essentially as 'a German problem'. Numerous attempts have already been made at providing a satisfactory analysis of the probable causal factors behind this trend, although an accurate diagnosis of the symptoms has not, as yet, been accompanied by any effective signs of a revival.[4] Indeed, despite underlying social changes of great significance and the rapid growth of the

* Notes are to be found at the end of the Editor's Introduction.

social sciences in Germany, the problems of adjustment
facing historians as a whole have been particularly difficult to assimilate in the general sphere of economic and
social history. The old-established tradition of German
historical writing, as incorporated in the figures of Friedrich Meinecke, George von Below and Heinrich von Sybel,
has maintained a surprising resilience throughout the
twentieth century. It is perhaps as if confronted by the
confusing enormity of the political and military catas-
trophes of this century, the rapid changes in social structure and the accompanying growth of the social sciences,
the historian alone, by retaining the analytical tools and
conceptual orientation of an earlier period, has been able
to provide for a wider public an important thread of continuity. The primacy of political history, however, and the
traditional methodology embodied in Ranke's famous
edict that all facts are equally important and that 'the
strictest presentation of the facts is the supreme law of
historiography' have effectively precluded an appraisal of
the possible benefits of new analytical techniques. Furthermore the spectre of the Marxist concept of 'historical
materialism' has served only to exaggerate the lag in the
replication within Germany of new developments in the
general sphere of historical research. To the extent that
many of these developments have stemmed from a growth
of interest in economic and social history, partly dependent on their comparative inter-relatedness with the
social sciences, the continued subjugation of these subject areas to the maintained traditionalism of 'Fachhistorie' has served merely to emphasise the process
of retardation within German historicism as a
whole.

The failure of German historians to respond adequately
to developments in the social sciences or to appraise the
prospective usefulness of advancements in the conceptual
and methodological fields is particularly ironic in the case
of economic history. Gustav Schmoller, as the main representative of the 'historical school' among German
economists of the late nineteenth century, embodied a
new relationship between historians, historical con-

sciousness and economists. Historical analysis was regarded as the 'foundation stone' for economic theory. Other contemporary economists, such as Roscher,[5] increasingly viewed history as the medium through which the laws of economic development could be delineated. Hildebrand, too, recognised the importance of statistics for historical research purposes, although perhaps the pioneer of the 'new economic history' of the nineteenth century was Karl Lamprecht, whose statistical approach marked a significant and distinctive break with traditional historical methods.[6] But perhaps the fate that overtook and engulfed this pioneering development of the late nineteenth century — which contained so much latent promise of an effective and productive link between history and economic theory — is symptomatic of the problems facing German historians today. Despite an initial upsurge of interest in Lamprecht's work and conceptual approach, which found practical expression in an increasing number of lectures and seminars on the 'social question' and German economic history at many universities during the early 1890s,[7] the attempted breakthrough proved abortive. The traditional school of political history, with its emphasis on such sacred tenets as 'free will' and the decisive role of personalities in historical development, was able, by means of its political influence and its effective control over the main historical journal, to reassert its position. Under the weight of the united opposition of such established figures as Max Lehmann, Felix Rachfahl, Heinrich Finke and above all Friedrich Meinecke, the attempted restructuring of the school of historicism along more empirical, economic and positivist lines was effectively emasculated. The aftermath of Versailles — which focussed attention on diplomatic issues and diplomatic history — and the growth of National Socialism finally ensured the continued longevity of the traditional school of German historicism. Even Schmoller's close links with economics were to prove of no avail in this context. His initiatives as a builder of interdisciplinary bridges finally tended to lose their impetus and direction and were dissipated along more

subsidiary lines of research, as for example in the examination of comparative economic systems (Sombart,
Weber, Eucken).[8] J. H. Clapham may have justifiably
claimed that '. . . economic history in its comprehensive
modern form and with its modern title had first grown in
the German speaking countries',[9] but perhaps the application of an 'early start hypothesis' may provide some
explanation for the increasing rigidity of much present-
day historical writing in Germany, particularly from the
point of view of the continued relative neglect of the possible contribution of economic and social history to the
central core of 'Fachhistorie'. If indeed this hypothesis
were applicable, it would also help to explain why the
'early starter' has consistently failed to maintain the
growth-rates of an earlier period.

It is in this context that Böhme's book is of some considerable importance.[10] Textbooks on the economic and
social history of Germany in the early modern and modern
periods are as a whole in short supply;[11] and when it first
appeared in 1968 it was regarded in some quarters as '. . .
refreshing in the conservative context of West German
historiography'.[12] It is conceived and designed as an
attempt to bridge the gap between traditional historical
explanation and modern economic theory, by examining
the contribution that theory – in the form of the business
cycle and Rostow's model of the stages of growth – can
possibly make to our understanding of German history.
The interconnection and interdependence of politics,
economic development and social structure are continuously emphasised; and this alone, as far as the past
pattern of historical writing is concerned, constitutes an
important step forward.

Böhme's work was not originally designed to serve in a
definitive role as a textbook of German economic and
social history, despite the relative paucity of general historical surveys of this kind even in the German language
itself. The aim of the study is rather to cast new light on the
inter-relationship between economics and politics in
moulding the development of Germany from the late
eighteenth century onwards. The central hypothesis is

that Germany's peculiar brand of industrialisation, to a large extent determined by the significant political compromise effected between the traditional agrarian interests of the feudal Prussian aristocracy on the one hand and the newly emergent body of industrialists, manufacturers and entrepreneurs on the other hand, bred irreconcilable political antagonisms. Although dormant for certain periods, these antagonisms were to erupt with ferocious intensity at other times and were to shape the overall path of German history. As a brief outline survey, therefore, Böhme's *Prolegomena* stands well outside the existing range of textbook material on German social and economic history, not only by virtue of its ability to incorporate concepts associated with the general body of economic theory, but also in the concise clarity of its exposition, which effectively serves to link together the different episodes of economic development in the various German territories into a comprehensible whole.

Indeed, such a synthesis of economic and social developments in the various parts of Germany during this period is particularly valuable and appropriate at this stage, in view of the signs of a new willingness among German historians to reappraise the evidence of the past with the help of new tools of analysis. There are still many spheres and facets of German historical development where the shadows of a past methodology tend to mask an effective appreciation of the causative factors behind the pattern of industrial growth and social change during the nineteenth and early twentieth centuries. But despite the continued absence of any degree of unanimity in relation to the actual dating of the 'take-off' in Germany,[13] the immediate period preceding the publication of Böhme's *Prolegomena* and the years which have followed have seen the appearance of a number of important works which collectively have widened the general understanding of the process of initial industrialisation in the various German territories.

On important aspect connected with the growing impetus of industrialisation relates to the mechanism of the replication of innovatory technologies. How was the 'industrial revolution' effectively transferred to the continent and in particular to Germany? What factors determined the overall pace of replication within the territorial boundaries of the various German states? How substantially did the different process of innovation dissemination influence the pattern and rate of industrialisation? Recent studies in this sphere[14] have largely tended to reinforce the emphasis on the importance of direct visits of a one-directional nature, with a constant stream of German civil servants, manufacturers, scientists and members of the nobility flocking to the cradle of the industrial revolution. Although the initial adoption of English achievements may have had only a limited effect, the long-term significance of this diffusion process cannot be doubted. Even in the mid-nineteenth century there were frequently very positive spin-offs from such visits. In 1843, for example, the Barmer Wittenstein set up the first hydraulic press and steam engine for silks and half-silk goods in Germany, following a visit to the United Kingdom. Bückler visited England in 1851 to examine flax-spinning techniques and shortly after his return to Germany founded the firm of Schoeller, Mevissen and Bückler. It would indeed appear that with the possible exception of the Jews, Germans were the most enthusiastic group of international travellers to be found in the nineteenth century.[15] But Braun's reassessment of the positive role of the various learned societies[16] has emphasised the need to re-examine and perhaps to modify the traditional model. Both in the context of the primary and secondary sectors in Germany, the learned societies acted as 'moderators' and disseminators of English innovations. Indeed, the maintenance of close personal contacts with similar bodies in England, such as the Society of Arts, enabled a rapid transference of ideas and inventions to take place. According to Dr. Johann Ulrich Pauli, the founder of the 'Patriotische Gesellschaft Hamburg' (1765), the Society of Arts had without any doubt led people '. . . out of the darkness', and the close similarity in the function of these institutions both in England and in Germany underlines the common purpose for which they were established. Certainly the traditional model for explaining the pace and spatial diffusion of technological innovation in the early, pre-conditions period of industrial development requires some degree of modification, which, one hopes, further studies may provide.

Equally in the sphere of the composition and long-term growth of German trade, both foreign and inter-state, a number of recent publications have once again placed in question certain traditional tenets which had previously been regarded as unassailable.[17] A reliable analysis of the nature and volume of German foreign trade has long been a high-priority requirement, given the known weakness in this respect of existing works.[18] Indeed, the foreign trade sector is of undeniable importance not only for the general understanding of the process of industrial growth, but also in the context of the 'capital shortage' thesis in the early decades of the nineteenth century, which has postulated that the general absence of capital for funding industrial development was aggravated by the negative trade balance in most areas of the foreign trading account. Of equal importance in this context is the comparative role of the Customs Union. Superficially the reduction of internal tariffs and custom barriers and the trend towards market integration appear as particularly vital elements in the overall promotion of trade and industrial growth.[19] But what in fact was the overall contribution of the Customs Union to the process of economic development within its member states? What evidence is there for its general promotion of both inter-state and foreign trade in the early stages of German industrialisation? Kutz's recent publication has gone a long way towards providing a solution to some of these particular problems. As a result, the long-term growth of German trade can be assigned with a large degree of certainty to the mid 1820s, a full decade before the actual foundation of the Customs Union. Furthermore, there is no evidence of a negative balance on the foreign trading account that could have contributed to a new outflow of capital from Germany. Although further studies of the economic impact of the Customs Union are still needed, particularly as far as inter-state flows of com-

modities, labour and capital are concerned, the contribution which it made to the initial promotion of foreign
trade in the early decades of the nineteenth century has
clearly been placed in a new and interesting perspective.
The traditional primacy of the role of the Customs Union
has effectively been placed in some doubt, and the doubts
initially voiced by Tilly in the context of the external
impact of the Customs Union in limiting foreign competition in Germany (particularly from cheap industrial
products from England)[20] have received support from
another source.

Within the general context of the problem of capital
accumulation and the evolution of an effective banking
mechanism, however, recent publications by Eistert and
Seeger[21] have added considerably to the general level of
knowledge in this sphere, particularly in relation to the
later decades of the nineteenth century, when German
industrial growth became very substantial indeed. On the
one hand confirmation has been provided of the limitations in the automatic adjustment mechanism of the
Gold Standard. As far as the Reichsbank was concerned,
its policies reveal a marked reluctance to accept the concept of non-intervention. The general rules of the Gold
Standard may have been accorded public recognition, but
in private they were flouted only too often. On the other
hand Eistert's important study has reaffirmed in quantifiable terms the positive contribution of the banking
mechanism to the overall performance of the German
economy in the period prior to 1914. Total net investment
in Germany rose from 642 million marks (1851–5) to 1,780
millions (1881–5) and finally to c.8,000 millions (1911–13).
The proportion of net investment financed by the banking
sector, however, having reached a low point of 16% in
1876–80 when its contribution was exceeded by the level
of public sector financing, rose significantly in the following years to reach a maximum of 43% in 1906–10. In
the case of Germany, therefore, quantifiable evidence has
now been provided to support a thesis that had long been
put forward by historians on the basis of a traditional
methodological approach. The credit policy of the bank-

ing system in Germany did actively promote industrial and economic growth in the latter part of the nineteenth century, when the ratio of funds made available (in the form of new advances) to national income rose annually by 1.8% (1885–95) to 6.2% (1895–1911).

Further, the general availability of adequate capital supplies for direct investment in the expanding secondary sector throughout the whole of the nineteenth century was probably substantially improved by the nature of most systems of taxation operating in the various states in Germany. Indirect taxation, which can actively assist individual capital accumulation, was prominent in most German states. Equally, the absence of any progressive taxation of income until the last two decades of the nineteenth century probably meant that during the crucial period of 'take-off' potential high savers were given command over a disproportionately large section of available resources on the basis of the regressive structure of the taxation system.[22] Furthermore Eckart Schremmer has shown that the introduction of the cadastral system of taxation in the early decades of the nineteenth century provided a direct incentive to the further accumulation of capital, particularly among manufacturers and handicraft producers located in rural areas.[23] At the same time, however, the general subject of taxation structure and policy is another area where further studies are really required before an overall picture of the inter-relationship between this particular variable and the overall process of industrial growth can be effectively delineated.

It is, however, in the discussion of the role of the leading sectors in the process of industrialisation in Germany that the most significant steps have as yet been taken in the utilisation and implementation of new techniques of analysis in the general field known as cliometrics. Holtfrerich in particular[24] has utilised a relatively sophisticated set of analytical tools to examine on a firmer basis one of the basic aspects of nineteenth-century economic development in Germany. The Hoffman-Landes hypothesis that coal-mining effectively constituted a leading sector in the crucial growth period of the German economy between 1851 and 1892 has received wide acceptance since its initial appearance. It is only with Holtfrerich's recent study, however, that this hypothesis has been subjected to a rigorous test. The basic Cobb-Douglas production function is applied to elucidate the causal factors which determined the rate of increased output in this crucial sector, and the inter-relationship of price movements and investment/production decisions on the part of the German entrepreneurs is highlighted by the application of the cobweb theorem. Finally, the actual role of coal-mining and the overall significance of the inter-sectoral linkages of this industry with the other important growth areas of industrial production in Germany are examined on the basis of the Leontief multiplier and a basic input-output analysis. The significance of the results obtained by these methods is considerable, and it provides a basis for testing the established criteria appropriate to the performance of a leading sector. Unfortunately, many of these established criteria appear applicable to all three possible leading sectors in Germany – coal-mining, railway construction and steel production. If the development of deep-pit mining involved something of a radical change in the production function in this particular sector, the same effect can be postulated for the development of large-scale railway construction and the adoption of coke-fired blast furnaces. Equally, all three sectors had an above-average rate of growth throughout the vital decades of the nineteenth century, and, in relation to their respective weighting factor in the economy as a whole, they all played a major role in determining the general process of industrial growth. All three prospective leading sectors had limited backward linkages, but very strong forward linkages, Indeed, only in relation to the final criterion deemed essential for a leading sector – namely its contribution to unbalanced growth that generates cobweb price and production patterns – can it be said that something like an ordered hierarchy emerges between the three major sectors under consideration. If the established time-lag between investment and increased output was noticeably longer in the coal-mining sector than in the case of the steel industry, the investment lag in the case of the railway sector was even greater, and it is upon this basis that railway construction is regarded as having been of the utmost economic importance in determining the overall pattern and pace of industrial growth in nineteenth century Germany: a decision which is supported by two further recent studies devoted exclusively to the performance of the railway construction sector.[25]

Significant advances have also been made in the field of historical demography in Germany, although this sphere is still largely synonymous with the work of Köllmann and Blaschke.[26] The degree to which the methodological advances associated with family reconstitution and record linkage have in fact been adopted in Germany nevertheless still leaves something to be desired, despite the work of von Nell on the structure of middle-class and peasant families which was largely based on extant geneological compilations.[27] At the same time, however, the significance of the population variable – both in the context of general social change and its interrelationship with the overal process of economic and industrial growth – has been clearly recognised in German historical circles. Peter Marschalk, for example, has provided an exemplary study of the movement of German overseas migration, which furthermore combines empirical research with the utilisation of theoretical models.[28] Phayer has even adopted some of the Anglo-French methodology connected with demographic history as a whole, to elucidate some of the changing social attitudes in Bavaria in the period 1750 to 1850.[29] Mauersberg's studies of the growth of urban centres such as Fulda and Fürth have inevitably touched upon the general significance of the population variable and population growth in the nineteenth century.[30] But by and large this general sphere remains like a newly-discovered continent the riches of which can only be revealed by the process of further exploration and investigation. To a large extent the impetus for change and development has come from foreign contributions, which have clearly shown the general applicability of modern methodology to the abundant source material available in most parts of Germany.[31] Many questions have still to be resolved, many problems have still to be posed, but a start has indeed been made. The transition from traditionalism to a more open approach for historical research, which Böhme rightly regards as being of the utmost importance for German historiography as a whole, is certainly already visible in this sphere. Symptomatic of this transition is Teuteberg's recent work on changes in diet and food consumption in Germany, a subject clearly of some significance, which many 'traditionalists' would scarcely have given any attention to at all.[32]

Finally a brief word is required in the context of recent developments in the sphere of research into the development of the primary sector. Indeed, the receptiveness of the school of economic history in Germany to modern theory is to some extent perhaps best illustrated by reference to this sector. As Böhme correctly points out, one of the first exponents of the concept of long cycles in Germany was the agricultural historian Abel.[33] This tradition of adaptability has been successfully maintained. The work of Schremmer, for example, reveals a sound grounding in economic theory which provides an insight into how future research in Germany could develop.[34] The matching of empirical research and economic theory has shed new light on a number of important questions bound up with the relative role of the primary sector in German nineteenth century development. The significance of rural-based craft production in influencing the process of industrialisation has been highlighted, and the contribution of the primary sector to capital accumulation has been underlined. Of course traditional, largely descriptive studies continue to appear, and these serve a useful role in expanding the level of overall knowledge and information in this sector; but it is from a synthesis of these results with economic theory that the most promising advances in agricultural history may be expected in the years to come.

To this extent the increasing sophistication of analytical methods in many areas of German historical research is already producing concrete benefits for the school of economic history as a whole. In part this is due to the increasing availability of statistical series[35] and partly a reflection of a new willingness to appraise the possibilities of modern analytical techniques. Economic theory, as such, is providing historians with the tools of research vitally necessary for the testing of important hypotheses,[36] which in many cases — partly by default, partly because of the continued influence of the traditional school — have become embedded in the infrastructure of accepted beliefs. Traditional assessments of the nature of German economic development and social change can therefore be re-examined in the light of the information that modern techniques provide.

It would of course be not only impossible, but also inappropriate to attempt to provide a full survey of recent trends in German economic and social history. The brief sketches provided are largely taken from publications relating to the nineteenth century; but nevertheless they do, as a whole, reinforce Böhme's purpose in writing the *Prolegomena*. German economic and social history is tentatively emerging from the comfort and warmth provided by the womb of traditionalism, which to a large extent has restricted its potential growth for so long. To the extent that Böhme's work seeks to bridge the chasm between traditional interpretation and modern theory, this general synthesis of Germany's development in the nineteenth and twentieth centuries provides a stimulus to further research. The portents are favourable, given a continued willingness to adapt developments in theory, whether economic or social, to the extant historical data.

As a work the *Prolegomena* has its limitations, but these are primarily dependent on the stated original purpose of the book. If there is no attempt to distinguish between independent and dependent variables, or to examine the 'axioms' of indispensability and counterfactual premises which are the hallmark of the 'new economic history', this is largely because such an exercise effectively lies outside the scope of the present work. Although at times a greater

degree of refinement would undoubtedly have improved
the qualitative basis of many of the ideas voiced in the
general analysis, as in the case of the much-disputed dating of the 'take-off' in Germany, the refreshingly open
approach to the general themes of German economic and
social history should make this work particularly valuable
for both the general reader and the student of German
development in the nineteenth and twentieth centuries.
Kindleberger once pinpointed one of the major problems
facing economic historians. 'Economic history, like all
history, is absorbing, beguiling, great fun. But for scientific purposes, can it be taken seriously?'[37] It is hoped
that Böhme's work may go some way to providing an
answer to this fundamental question. At the same time it
will possibly reinforce the slow, but increasingly significant trend of examining some of the more established
'truths' of German economic development by means of the
analytical tools which the social sciences are making
increasingly available to historians. It is now up to the
practitioners of the profession in Germany itself to utilise
these tools in a positive and constructive way. Clearly,
many possible areas of activity and research exist which
would be suited to the application of economic theory.
Sectoral monograph studies for individual industries are
seriously needed to provide a microanalytical basis for the
general study of the process of industrialisation in Germany. Equally little has so far been written on the performance of different branches of the economy in the present century, and specifically for the post-1945 period.
Although traditional business history is already well
served by the journal publication *Tradition**, which
deserves wider recognition outside Germany,[38] there are
many areas which still require an effectively wider treatment. Little is known about the growth of public utilities,[39]
of gas and electric companies, of the process of horizontal
and vertical integration, of product diversification or even
the evolution of individual firms. Equally the significance
of the residual and the contribution of technical education
requires further investigation in the context of individual

* Now renamed as the Zeitschrift für Unternehmensgeschichte.

sectors of industry.[40] The strand of mercantilist or neo-mercantilist intervention on the part of the state is visible both in the nineteenth and twentieth centuries. But what was the economic effect of government policies? How can the effective contribution of the state to the general process of economic growth in Germany be quantified? On balance the weight of existing studies has tended to be concentrated on areas of rapid industrial growth, such as the Ruhr, Saxony and Silesia. Perhaps it is also apposite at this juncture to press for the focussing of attention on more backward areas such as Bavaria, where industrialisation only became significant in the course of the present century. Such a shift in emphasis could only serve to provide a greater insight into the causative factors determining the process of industrial development during this period. Was the concentration of secondary sector growth in certain areas of Germany determined solely by resource allocation? Or perhaps the focal location of growth areas within the different and diverse German states was influenced by more structural factors, such as the different systems of taxation, land inheritance and the nature of local society. What light does modern social theory shed on the determinants of entrepreneurial behaviour and investment decisions? How can the use of demographic techniques effectively be implemented to cast light on the net contribution of the population variable to the process of German economic growth? Perhaps the problem lies in the very multiplicity of areas which still require examination and the diversity of the questions that modern economic and social historians can pose. But if Böhme's work can be said to have stimulated the general process of further enquiry, by emphasising the nature of the interrelationship between political, economic and social development in Germany, then the publication's original purpose will have been served and German historians will have received a further impetus in the right direction which may hopefully enable them to meet the modern challenge, which as formulated by Wolfram Fischer, was to acquire a greater precision in the formulation of questions and an improved ability to handle problems of

Editor's Introduction .

economic causality.[41] Only perhaps by undergoing this process of development will it be possible for the German historical school to master its ever-imminent crisis and achieve once again a period of 'self-sustained' growth.

Robert Lee
UNIVERSITY OF LIVERPOOL

Notes to Editor's Introduction

1. J. H. Plumb (ed.), *Crisis in the Humanities*. London: 1964, p. 44.
2. R. Koselleck. 'Wozu noch Historie?' in *Historische Zeitschrift*. Band 212: 1971, p. 1.
3. F. Stern, 'Rationalismus und Irrationalismus in Deutschland (Arbeitsgruppenbericht)' in *Aufklärung heute — Probleme der deutschen Gesellschaft*. Freiburg: 1967, p. 57.
4. G. G. Iggers, *Deutsche Geschichtswissenschaft. Eine Kritik der traditionellen Geschichtsauffassung von Herder bis zur Gegenwart*. München: 1971. A. Loesdau, 'Die Interpretation der Krise der bürgerlichen Geschichtsschreibung durch G. G. Iggers,' in *Das Argument*, No. 75, Berlin: 1972. W. Köllmann, 'Zur Situation des Faches Sozial-und Wirtschaftsgeschichte in Deutschland' in K-H. Manegold (ed.), *Wissenschaft, Wirtschaft und Technik, Studien zur Geschichte*. München: 1969, pp. 135–46.
5. W. Roscher, *Die Geschichte der National-ökonomie in Deutschland*. München: 1874.
6. K. Lamprecht, *Deutsche Wirtschaftsleben im Mittelalter*, 4 vols. Leipzig: 1886. Ibid, 'Deutsches Städteleben am Schluss des Mittelalters,' in *Sammlung von Vorträgen*. W. Frommel and A. Pfaffe (eds.), Band XII: 1879. Ibid, *Deutsche Geschichte*. 14 Bde., Berlin: 1891–1909.
7. G. Oestreich, 'Die Fachhistorie und die Anfänge der sozialgeschichtlichen Forschung in Deutschland', in *Historische Zeitschrift*. Band 208: 1969, p. 332.
8. G. Schmölders, *Geschichte der Volkswirtschaftslehre*. München (first edition 1962): 1970, p. 70.
9. J. H. Clapham, 'Economic History, Survey of Development to the Twentieth Century,' in *Encyclopaedia of the Social Sciences*. New

York: 1931, Vol. 5, p. 318. Cited in K. W. Hardach, 'Some remarks on German Economic Historiography and its Understanding of the Industrial Revolution in Germany,' in *The Journal of European Economic History*. Vol. 1, No. 1: 1972, p. 37.

10. H. Böhme, *Prolegomena zu einer Sozial- und Wirtschaftsgeschichte Deutschlands im 19. und 20. Jahrhundert*. Suhrkamp Verlag (fourth edition), Frankfurt am Main: 1972. (First published 1968).

11. A. Sartorius von Waltershausen, 'Deutsche Wirtschaftsgeschichte, 1815–1914', Jena, 1920. W. Treue, 'Wirtschafts- und Sozialgeschichte Deutschlands im 19. Jahrhundert', in *Handbuch der deutschen Geschichte*. B. Gebhardt (ed.), Vol. III., Stuttgart: 1960. H. Bechtel, *Wirtschafts- und Sozialgeschichte Deutschlands*, Munich: 1967 (previously published in 3 volumes, 1951–6). G. Stolper, K. Häuser and K. Borchardt, *Deutsche Wirtschaft seit 1870*. Tübingen: 1966. F. Lütge, *Deutsche Sozial- und Wirtschaftsgeschichte*. Berlin: 1966. R. Engelsing, *Kleine Wirtschafts- und Sozialgeschichte Deutschlands*. Hanover: 1968. K. Borchardt, 'The Emergence of Industrial Society in Germany, 1700–1918', in *The Fontana Economic History of Europe*. C. M. Cipolla (ed.), Vol. 4, part 1: London, 1973. H. Mottek, *Wirtschaftsgeschichte Deutschlands*. 3 volumes, Berlin: 1968, 1969, 1974 (the third volume in conjunction with W. Becker and A. Schröter). W. O. Henderson, *The Rise of German Industrial Power, 1834–1914*. London: 1975.

12. R. H. Tilly. ' "Soll und Haben" : Recent German Economic History and the problems of Economic Development', in *Journal of Economic History*. Vol. 29: 1969, p. 300.

13. The diversity in the exact dating of 'take-off' in Germany is certainly quite substantial. W. G. Hoffmann ('The Take-off in Germany' in *The Economics of Take-off into Sustained Growth*. W. W. Rostow (ed.), London: 1963, pp. 95–118.) has argued that the period of effective economic and industrial growth in Germany only began after the period 1855–60. W. O. Henderson (*The Zollverein*. Cambridge: 1939, p. 338), on the other hand, envisages the general period 1815–71 as constituting the 'genesis of the industrial revolution' in Germany. Equally, if J. Kuczynski (*Darstellung der Lage der Arbeiter in Deutschland von 1789 bis 1849*. Berlin: 1961, p. 87.) can argue that the turning-point in the evolution of economic production must be placed in the latter decades of the eighteenth century (c. 1785), Knut Borchardt ('Grundriss der deutschen Wirtschaftsgeschichte', in *Kompendium der Volkswirtschaftslehre*. W. Ehrlicher *et al.* (eds.), Vol. I, Göttingen: 1967, p. 368.) by stressing the acceptability of either the 1830s, 1840s or 1850s as a suitable take-off date comes far closer to mirroring the increasing consensus among German historians that these decades of the nineteenth century were by and large of crucial importance for the overall development of the German

Notes to Editor's Introduction

economy. For a further discussion of this issue, reference can be made to K. W. Hardach, *op. cit.*, pp. 53–70.

14. M. Schuhmacher, 'Auslandsreisen deutscher Unternehmer, 1750–1851, Unter besonderer Berücksichtigung von Rheinland und Westfalen', *Schriften zur Rheinisch-Westfälischen Wirtschaftsgeschichte*. Vol. 17, Köln: 1968. W. Kroker, *Wege zur Verbreitung technologischer Kenntnisse zwischen England und Deutschland in der zweiten Hälfte des 18. Jahrhunderts*. Berlin: 1971.

15. 'Der Reisende. Ein Wochenblatt zur Ausbreitung gemeinnüzziger Kenntnisse, 10. 4. 1782. Hamburg'. Cited in M. Schuhmacher, *op. cit.*, p. 6.

16. H-J. Braun, *Technologische Beziehungen zwischen Deutschland und England von der Mitte des 17. bis zum Ausgang des 18. Jahrhunderts*. Verlag Schwann, Düsseldorf: 1974.

17. B. von Borries, 'Deutschlands Aussenhandel, 1836–1856. Eine statistische Untersuchung zur Frühindustrialisierung', in *Forschungen zur Sozial- und Wirtschaftsgeschichte*. Vol. 13, Stuttgart: 1970. M. Kutz, 'Deutschlands Aussenhandel von der Französischen Revolution bis zur Gründung des Zollvereins. Eine statistische Strukturuntersuchung zur vorindustriellen Zeit', in *Vierteljahrschrift für Sozial- und Wirtschaftsgeschichte*. Beiheft No. 61, Wiesbaden: 1974. Kaufhold, in his article 'Das preussische Handwerk in der Zeit der Frühindustrialisierung, Beiträge zu Wirtschaftswachstum und Wirtschaftsstruktur im 16. und 19. Jahrhundert' (in W. Fischer [ed.], Berlin: 1971 pp. 169–193), also sketches the general development tendencies of various trades during the period of early industrialisation, on the basis of Prussian trade statistics.

18. G. Bondi, 'Deutschlands Aussenhandel, 1815–1870'. Berlin: 1958 (Schriften des Instituts für Geschichte, Band 5.).

19. This is a view expressed in most existing textbooks, although the only monograph study on the Customs Union (W. O. Henderson, *op. cit.*, new impression London: 1968.) does not attempt to evaluate its effective economic impact.

20. R. H. Tilly, 'Los von England: Probleme des Nationalismus in der deutschen Wirtschaftsgeschichte', in *Zeitschrift für die gesamte Staatswissenschaft*. Vol. 124, Tübingen: 1968.

21. E. Eistert, *Die Beeinflussung des Wirtschaftswachstums in Deutschland von 1883 bis 1913 durch das Bankensystem. Eine theoretisch-empirische Untersuchung*. Berlin: 1970. M. Seeger, 'Die Politik der Reichsbank von 1876–1914 im Licht der Spielregeln der Geldwährung, in *Volkswirtschaftliche Schriften*. Heft 125, Berlin: 1968.

22. W. R. Lee, 'Tax Structure and Economic Growth in Germany (1750–1850)', *in The Journal of European Economic History*. Vol. 4, No. 1: 1975, pp. 153–178.

28. E. Schremmer, 'Zusammenhänge zwischen Katastersteuerersystem,

Notes to Editor's Introduction

Wirtschaftswachstum und Wirtschaftsstruktur im 19. Jahrhundert', Das Beispiel Württemberg: 1821–1877/1903; in *Festschrift für Wilhelm Abel zum 70. Geburtstag. Schriftenreihe für ländliche Sozialfragen.* Heft 70, Hannover: 1974, pp. 679–706.

24. C-L. Holtfrerich, *Quantitative Wirtschaftsgeschichte des Ruhrkohlenbergbaus im 19. Jahrhundert.* Dortmund: 1973.
25. H. Wagenblass, 'Der Eisenbahnbau und das Wachstum der deutschen Eisen- und Maschinenindustrie, 1835–1860', in *Forschungen zur Sozial-und Wirtschaftsgeschichte.* Vol. 18, Stuttgart: 1973. R. Fremdling, *Eisenbahnen und deutsches Wirtschaftswachstum, 1840–1879. Ein Beitrag zur Entwicklungstheorie und zur Theorie der Infrastruktur.* Dortmund: 1975.
26. K. Blaschke, *Zur Bevölkerungsgeschichte Sachsens vor der industriellen Revolution,* in E. Giersiepen and D. Lösche (eds.), *Beiträge zur deutschen Wirtschafts-und Sozialgeschichte des 18. und 19. Jahrhunderts.* Berlin: 1962, pp. 133–170. *Ibid., Bevölkerungsgeschichte von Sachsen bis zur industriellen Revolution.* Weimar: 1967. W. Köllmann, *Grundzüge der Bevölkerungsgeschichte Deutschlands im 19. und 20. Jahrhundert.* Studium Generale: 1959. *Ibid.,* 'The Population of Barmen before and during the period of Industrialisation', in *Population in History.* D. V. Glass and D. E. C. Eversley (eds.), London: 1965, pp. 558–607. *Ibid.,* 'Bevölkerung in der Industriellen Revolution', *Kritische Studien zur Geschichtswissenschaft.* Band 12, Göttingen: 1974.
27. A. von Nell, 'Die Entwicklung der generativen Strukturen bürgerlicher und bäuerlicher Familien von 1750 bis zur Gegenwart'. Diss. rer. soc. Bochum: 1973.
28. P. Marschalk, *Deutsche Uebersee wanderung im 19. Jahrhundert. Ein Beitrag zur soziologischen Theorie der Bevölkerung.* Stuttgart: 1973.
29. F. M. Phayer, 'Religion und das Gewöhnliche Volk in Bayern in der Zeit von 1750–1850', *Miscellanea Bavarica Monacensia.* Heft 21, München: 1970.
30. H. Mauersberg, *Die Wirtschaft und Gesellschaft Fuldas in neuerer Zeit.* Göttingen: 1969. *Ibid., Wirtschaft und Gesellschaft Fürths in neuer und neuester Zeit.* Göttingen: 1974.
31. J. E. Knodel, 'Infant mortality and fertility in three Bavarian villages', in *Population Studies. Vol. 21., No. 3. Ibid.* (with E. van de Walle)., 'Breast feeding, fertility and infant mortality: an analysis of some early German data', in *Population Studies.* Vol. 21.: 1967, pp. 109–131. *Ibid.,* 'Two and a half Centuries of Demographic History in a Bavarian Village', *Population Studies,* 1972. *Ibid., The decline of Fertility in Germany, 1871–1939.* Princeton University Press, Princeton: 1974. W. R. Lee, 'Zur Bevölkerungsgeschichte Bayerns, 1750–1850: Britische Forschungsergebnisse', in *Vierteljahrschrift für Sozial- und Wirtschaftsgeschichte.* Band 62, Heft 3: 1975, pp. 309–338.
32. H.-J. Teuteberg. 'Variations in meat consumption in Germany', in

Ethnologia Scandinavica. A Journal for Nordic Ethnology, 1971.
Ibid. (with G. Wiegelmann), *Wandel der Nährungsgewohnheiten unter dem Einfluss der Industrializierung*. Göttingen: 1971.
33. H. Böhme, *op. cit.*, p. 11. A. Abel, *Geschichte der deutschen Landwirtschaft vom Mittelalter bis zum 19. Jahrhundert.* Stuttgart: 1962. *Ibid., Agrarkrise und Agrarkonjunktur.* Hamburg: 1966.
34. E. Schremmer, 'Standortausweitung der Warenproduktion im langfristigen Wirtschaftswachstum', in *Vierteljahrschrift für Sozial-und Wirtschaftsgeschichte.* Band 59, Heft I: 1972. *Ibid.*, 'Die Veränderung der Produktionsstruktur auf dem flachen Land im 17. und 18. Jahrhundert in Südostdeutschland', in *Proceedings of the Hungarian Agricultural Museum*, 1971—72. I. Wollman (ed.), Budapest: 1973, pp. 213–222. *Ibid.*, 'Ueberlegungen zur Bestimmung des gewerblichen und des agrarischen Elements in einer Region. Fragen und Probleme – auch zum Thema der Werturteile, in H. L. Kellenbenz (ed.), *Agrarisches Nebengewerbe und Formen der Reagrisierung im Spätmittelalter und 19/20 Jahrhundert. Forschungen zur Sozial- und Wirtschaftsgeschichte*, Bd. 21, Stuttgart: 1975.
35. R. Wagenführ, *Die Industriewirtschaft, Entwicklungstendenzen der deutschen und internationalen Industrieproduktion, 1866–1932.* Berlin: 1933. A. Jacobs and H. Richter, *Die Grosshandelspreise in Deutschland von 1792 bis 1934.* Berlin: 1935. W. G. Hoffmann (and J. H. Müller), *Das deutsche Volkseinkommen, 1851—1957.* Tübingen: 1959. *Ibid., Das Wachstum der deutschen Wirtschaft seit der Mitte des 19. Jahrhunderts.* Berlin: 1965. G. Helling, 'Berechnung eines Index der Agrarproduktion im 19. Jahrhundert', in *Jahrbuch für Wirtschaftsgeschichte.* Heft IV, Berlin: 1965. A situation will eventually be reached where most of the necessary statistical information will be available in easy form for the various German territories. Comparative statistical surveys also have a role to play in this particular context (e.g. B. R. Mitchell, *European Historical Statistics, 1750—1970.* London: 1975).
36. A number of important works incorporating advanced economic theory have already appeared, including the following publications. E. von Knorring, 'Die Berechnung makroökonomischer Konsumfunktionen für Deutschland, 1851–1913', in *Schriften zur angewandten Wirtschaftsforschung.* Band 29, Tübingen: 1970. R. H. Tilly, 'Zeitreihen zum Geldumlauf in Deutschland, 1870–1913', in *Jahrbücher für Nationalökonomie und Statistik.* Band 187/4: 1973. Distinctive developments in this general sphere have, however, often been linked with the influence of individual professors at specific universities, such as Tilly at Münster and Schremmer at Heidelberg. In the later case, two recent publications have confirmed the positive response of economic historians in Germany to new overall trends: W-R. Ott, 'Grundlageninvestitionen in Württemberg. Massnahmen zur Verbesserung der materiellen

Notes to Editor's Introduction

Infrastruktur in der Zeit vom Beginn des 19. Jahrhunderts bis zum Ende des ersten Weltkrieges', dissertation, Heidelberg: 1971; and H. Loreth, 'Das Wachstum der Württembergischen Wirtschaft von 1818 bis 1918', dissertation, Heidelberg: 1974.

37. C. P. Kindleberger, *Economic Growth in France and Britain, 1851–1950*. Cambridge, Massachusetts: 1964, p. 322.
38. 'Tradition', *Zeitschrift für Firmengeschichte und Unternehmer-biographie*. Edited by W. Treue.
39. H-J. Teuteberg, 'Anfänge kommunaler Stromversorgung – dargestellt am Beispiel Hamburg', in *Wissenschaft, Wirtschaft und Technik. Studien zur Geschichte. Wilhelm Treue zum 60. Geburtstag*. K-H. Manegold (ed.), München: 1969, pp. 363–78.
40. K–H. Manegold, *Universität, Technische Hochschule und Industrie. Ein Beitrag zur Emanzipation der Technik im 19. Jahrhundert*. Berlin: 1969.
41. W. Fischer, 'Oekonomische und soziologische Aspekte der frühen Industrialisierung', in *Wirtschafts-und Sozialgeschichtliche Probleme der frühen Industrialisierung*. W. Fischer (ed.), Berlin: 1968, p. 12.

Author's Introduction

This study has no intention of serving as a general historical portrayal, nor can it be a historical textbook of German economic and social history. It is simply an attempt within the framework of an exposition of the modern theories of the business cycle and economic growth to reconsider the main features of German social and economic history. It will utilise extant records from official administrative bodies within the individual states and in the Empire, as well as documents from individual firms in the private sector and those generated by the activities of political parties and trade unions. A conscious decision was made to omit an explanation of structural changes, the course of the business cycle and the movement of the economy as a whole, dependent on numerical representation and diagrams. In contrast to this type of approach a chronological account which incorporates an analysis of the interconnections of individual economic and social events, has been chosen.

Equally, this study does not attempt to present the multiple manifestations of the 'economy' and 'society'. On the contrary, the primary concern was to sketch with only a few strokes the technical and social changes which have taken place since the great upheaval at the beginning of the nineteenth century. Political developments have had

Introduction

to be largely excluded from the picture. Nevertheless, I have taken pains to direct attention again and again to the interconnection between politics, the economy and society, for without prior knowledge of this element of interdependence, it is impossible to evaluate the basic nature of both the technical and economic revolution as well as the revolutionary developments in society and in the state.

This study would probably never have appeared without the initiation into the problems of interpreting the modern German state which I received from my teacher, Professor Fritz Fischer. This book is dedicated to him, in veneration and with thanks.

H.B.   *Hamburg, January 1968*

xxx

*Great conquerors will always be gazed
at in wonderment and history will be
tailored according to their periods.
This is sad, but it is probably due to
human nature. . . . At a cattle market
everyone's attention is always focussed
on the biggest and fattest oxen.*

Georg Christoph Lichtenberg

1

Backwardness: the Tradition of German Development

At the end of the eighteenth century, about 1800 customs barriers hindered trading relations in central Europe. In Prussia alone there were 67 local customs tariffs and just as many customs borders. Import, export and transit dues, and in particular import and export prohibitions, helped to protect rigorously indigenous production and formed the most important basis for a mercantilist economic policy oriented to fiscal criteria. The main aim of such a policy was to guarantee the social and political order of the larger of the 314 sovereign imperial territories and the 1,475 imperial knights whose world was governed by the infrastructure provided by the Holy Roman Empire of the German nation. The conglomeration of extremely small and semi-autarchic markets corresponded to both the political situation of the Empire and to the needs of a society already strongly differentiated but still retaining intact an estate structure where individual classes were sharply distinguished from each other. The court, the nobility, the estate owners, the officer class and the leading families of the free urban bourgeoisie were the decisive elements in this old German world. They were served by a broad group of subordinate officials and a peasantry divided on the basis of the existing agricultural order by bonds of serfdom and seigneurial and judicial lordship. The social structure also included a growing group of householders and lodgers who had no legal rights and a craft and trading sector divided according to guilds. With four-fifths of the population still employed in the primary sector or dependent on agriculture, Germany was characterised by an almost completely agrarian structure, and in comparison with England and Western Europe had been involved only to a slight degree in the technical changes and revolutionary pressures that emerged towards the end of the eighteenth century.

Admittedly this land, situated in the centre of Europe, with its eighteen to twenty million inhabitants, possessed considerable economic potential. But poor roads, even if suited for through traffic, precluded the use of its advantageous geographical position. West and East Prussia, for example, had no firm highways; and in the western provinces of Prussia, separated moreover from the rest by a customs frontier, there were only two short man-made roads. Equally adverse factors were the extensive distances between the individual manufacturing and production centres, and unregulated waterways and shallow canals, both of which restricted the benefits that could be drawn from its rich mineral resources and primary raw materials. Politically divided, Germany had no chance to build up a large market organisation. Certainly there were market cities, such as Frankfurt and Leipzig, which served as transit stations for European trade and as bases for German transit and export trade; certainly there were ports which acted as intermediaries for German trading interests. But Emden was Prussian, Bremen, Lübeck and Hamburg were free cities, Rostock belonged to Mecklenburg, Wismar was Swedish, and the Prussian ports of Stettin, Königsberg and Memel were isolated by inter-state customs barriers. Wood, stone, grain, fish and iron were imported from Scandinavia; southern fruits, oil and wine from Portugal, Spain and Italy; manufactured goods, coal and salt from Great Britain; wine, brandy and luxury goods from France; furs and raw materials from Russia; and cotton from Central and North America. Yet the turnover, compared to that of England, was slight, and the German exports of metals, pig-iron, copper, lead, zinc ore, metal products, stones, clay, slate, wood and textile products formed only a minute proportion of the imported luxury goods. For example, about the turn of the century German exports to England probably amounted to a sixth of the imports from that country. Certainly at that time Germany did possess certain distinguished manufacturing centres, including Augsburg, Schwäbisch Gmünd, Hanau and Pforzheim for gold and silverware, Nürnberg, Stolberg and Iserlohn for copper and tin goods, Suhl and Ruhla for the manufacture of weapons and the Hunsrück for the production of cast-iron. Gladbach, Rheydt, Krefeld, Berlin, Magdeburg, Halle and Erlangen had reputations as cotton manufacturing cities and producers of silk and velvet goods, but the quantities produced were small and the market was restricted to a very small section of noble customers with exclusive needs and interests. As there was no general consumer demand, in contrast to England, the necessary prerequisites for the introduction of technological innovation were lacking. As a result the objective conditions for the development of a self-conscious, homogeneous work-force were also absent. The social and economic position of the German working class was marked by an extremely high degree of differentiation in their pay scales (W. Fischer), which, in contrast to the situation in England, helped to preserve the estate tradition into the nineteenth century. The general mass of the population was poor. The dependent serfs on the feudal estates in the provinces east of the Elbe were not the only ones who lived off salted herrings when times were good. How a clerk in Prussia with an annual income of 50 Taler could make ends meet even if he and his family maintained a diet consisting largely of bread and water soup and potatoes, it is impossible to know (Wilhelm Abel). And yet even those who received top salaries, often earning sixty times the salary of an average official, could indeed enjoy a secure life, albeit one that precluded all luxuries. This group of leading officials, at the same time, was quite separated from the broad mass of the population on the land and in the few cities. At the turn of the century

3

in Berlin – which with Hamburg was the only city on German territory with over 100,000 inhabitants – every fourth or fifth inhabitant could no longer satisfy his or her elementary economic needs from indigenous resources even according to the strictest reckoning of minimum subsistence requirements. No trade could be conducted with these groups in the population and they provided no incentive for the financing of investments. Such living conditions were typical both in Prussia and in Württemberg, although because of the effective division of landed holdings conditions in the South were even more pitiful than in the East, which is traditionally described in the literature as 'backward'. As a result, the strong economic demands generated by the capital cities of Munich, Stuttgart, Würzburg, Ansbach, Bamberg, Erlangen, Dresden, Kassel, Hanover and Berlin found expression only in foreign trading accounts. Regarded as economic data, the balances of German commodity trade of that period have no explanatory value. Indeed, it was above all foreign trade which met the needs of the few great fairs, the ports and local staple towns, and of the small number of merchant families in the individual cities.

Nevertheless, the capital cities did play an important role in the history of economic development. Despite the great variety in the political ambitions of individual German territories and despite all the peculiarities of inherited tradition, it was only from these centres that the impulse emerged which led at the end of the eighteenth century to an increase in productivity both in agriculture and manufacturing, and which was quite considerable by continental standards. At the same time it must be noted that economic development in Germany was always a state matter and therefore, it corresponded to the ideas and the needs of the leading classes. Even the small manufacturing concerns scattered over the whole Empire, partly bourgeois, partly Jewish and partly feudal in origin (which functioned, for example, in Krefeld, Wuppertal, Solingen and Remscheid as family concerns and without state help) did not constitute an exception to this general rule. Without the support of banks, without consolidated and secure land and water transport communications, in the absence of insurance firms, restricted by a fiscal customs policy based on the smallest political units, and without any general marketing possibilities, they too were dependent on the wishes and directives of the state, its officials, its military establishment, its court and its cities, which simply served as supply and administrative centres.

The traditional German economy, organised according to the idea of the communal, 'complete house', can therefore be understood only in terms of the unity between state and society. The fatherly principle of welfare, and not that of profit maximisation, determined the economic activity of the subjects and helped to preserve the traditional honourable order. The individual was seen as a member of a family, and of the state organisation, with the ruler as the caring sovereign at the head of the res publica sive societas civilis.[1] A concentration of workers in a factory system and their separation from the structure of a feudal Christian world would have been inconceivable. Granted, people knew about the domestic system and the division of different parts of the work process between different workers, but the workers and the work process itself remained within the confines of the traditional extended family. The utilisation of the labour force according to utility and solely from the point of view of gaining the greatest profit from labour had still not become the general rule. Even child and female labour was still regarded as part of the concept of provisioning the family. The search for profit and personal prosperity still did not count as one of the most decisive motives behind economic activity. The tradition was still that of princely care and gracious benevolence. For this reason the noticeable population pressure evident in central Europe at about the turn of the century failed to act as the cause of economic change, or as the impetus towards new production and retailing organisations. The state, based on an estate structure, remained unaffected, and so with it the traditional social and economic order.

1. 'The State or the fellowship of citizens'.

The Tradition of German Development

The total change in the position of the individual in the system of economic organisation, which was particularly prominent in England around the mid-eighteenth century, and the substitution of human labour by machines and primary raw materials by mineral products, had little noticeable effect in Germany. The skilful merchant and the manufacturer, even if they already existed, could not 'rule' there, as in England. Other traditions remained predominant on the Continent. The estate society still stood in an impregnable position and did not appear to be threatened, despite the dynamic tendencies revealed by the expansion of population and economic production. The village had its predetermined number of tenements and peasants, and the situation in the city was equally stable. Corporations, guilds, seigneurial and judicial lordship guaranteed an order, the stability of which rested effectively on the closed, corporative constitution of the state and in which the level of the available food supply, custom and work productivity represented the boundaries for the possible establishment of families. The growth in income was also necessarily limited to small groups, whose need for clothing, food and accommodation, etc., was so slight in the economic sense that no market could have been established, which would have created new demand and new employment possibilities. The result of this was a steady deterioration in the position of the under-privileged and in particular of the smallholders and impoverished classes who had no legal rights and for whom there was no place, either in the expanding agricultural sector, in the administration, or in industry. General purchasing power remained weak and unstable, and the economy continued as before to draw on the natural sources of raw materials.

But this certainly did not mean that Germany remained completely cut off from English innovation. The first mechanical spinning factory, for example, was founded in 1784 near Ratingen. The first German steam engine was put into use in 1785 in the Mansfeld mining district. The first German coal-fired blast furnace was erected in 1794/96 in Upper Silesia in Gleiwitz, and in 1799 the

Königshütte became the second establishment to possess a blast furnace. All these adoptions of English achievements, however, remained in the majority of cases expensive experiments, museum pieces that represented the tradition of the baroque art of machine building. They were in any case the expression of state rather than private initiative. As a result their influence on the economic processes remained limited. Production towards the end of the eighteenth century still continued to be clearly dependent on the needs of princely armaments concerns and the manufacture of textiles, porcelain, glass and iron. In England, on the other hand, by the end of the eighteenth century the boundaries had already been surpassed, which for thousands of years had effectively set limits on the extent of human labour. This had been achieved by inventions in the textile industry and later in the sphere of the iron, machine and chemical industries, and by the introduction and utilization of new machines and sources of energy. It had also been accompanied by the development of new techniques, by a transformation in the conditions of production, the construction of canals and transport routes and the reorganisation of markets. The Continent, however, continued with the old forms and the traditional household and family economy. The Continental economy could not match the 13–14% increase in the demand for wool in England during the years 1740 to 1770; and the rise in English imports of raw cotton from 2½ million lbs in 1760 to 22 million lbs in 1787 would only be experienced in Germany a full two generations later.

On the basis of these and other factors, the economic and social conditions in Germany at that time have been regarded as underdeveloped. Germany could only point to limited investments in the transport and raw materials sector. It possessed no general banking system and was devoid of any marked evidence of urbanisation or a rapid growth in productivity. It did not show any change in relative income distribution and possessed no large scale production. Although there had been a hesitant upswing in productivity and in the volume of trade from 1740

The Tradition of German Development

onwards, and although Germany had experienced a 'particularly hectic first foundation period' (H. Kellenbenz) about 1800 and an impressive 'increase of investments in the public and private sectors' (H. Rosenberg), compared with the technical and economic changes in England, the German development showed hardly any trace of an industrial revolution. On the other hand, it is doubtful whether the term underdeveloped can sufficiently characterise the situation in Germany at the beginning of the nineteenth century, because in a conceptual form this implies a completely fixed theory. Although the explanatory value of the theory, as a model, is well known, it runs the risk of not giving sufficient weight to economic and social developments as historical processes. It represents the doctrine of the sequence of economic stages, at the basis of which is the concept of economic inevitability. It goes back to the older historical school of List, Roscher, Bucher and Marx and was revived and more sharply defined by W. W. Rostow, but it is to a large extent independent of the specific historical individuality of the separate state. According to this interpretation, economic growth occurs under all conditions in the same way, although not contemporaneously in all cases. Underdevelopment, as it was understood by Rostow, meant a stage preliminary to industrialisation. The pre-conditions for an economic upswing at the beginning of the nineteenth century were not fulfilled in Germany, because the 'boundary of productivity was still determined by the production techniques applied' (W. W. Rostow). For this reason, Rostow concluded, there was no real alternative at this juncture to the traditional social structure. Only with the application of state investment, the emergence of a new type of entrepreneur and the adoption of new techniques of production, did domestic and foreign trade begin to flourish and changes in society become apparent. The economic upswing became discernible as soon as 'the proportion of effective investment and savings rose from let us say, 5% of National Income to 10% or more' (W. W. Rostow) and the stage of maturity is characterised by a continuous investment of 10–20% of National Income.

8

About sixty years after the beginnings of industrial change this position was reached in Germany.

Hence a bridge can be built to facilitate the introduction of a second no less fascinating, explanatory model of economic growth, which similarly has only recently been applied to the portrayal of historical developments. This is the doctrine that long-term fluctuations in the economy and the business cycles are basic categories of economic processes. Arthur Spiethoff, N. D. Kondratieff, C. A. R. Wardwell and Joseph Schumpeter, as well as Simon Kuznets, are the names which are above all connected with the different forms of this theory of long-term swings. Whereas the growth theorists seek to determine the secular character of modern economic growth, the business cycle theorists concentrate their efforts on the systematisation and representation of the oscillations around the trend, on the cyclical upswings and downswings of economic behaviour. Both theories are dependent on a highly-developed system of data abstraction and verification, and both have in common the fact that they claim to recognise a basic rhythm of economic growth in a sixty-year cycle, despite the varying emphases on the length of the swing. For example, Rostow's 'epoch of advancement' corresponds with Kondratieff's cycle, which lasts from 1789 until 1897 and is subdivided into an upswing to 1873 and a downswing until 1896. From the point of view of the historian, both theories have a great weakness in their insufficient consideration of the individual historical process as a phenomenon not completely quantifiable and comparable. It is doubtful, for example, whether the chronological postponement of industrial development in a country is nothing more than an external matter that has no repercussions on the industrial changes which occur later. It is perhaps equally plausible, according to Alexander Gerschenkron, that the individual trends of industrial development are completely determined by the backwardness of a country. Alternatively as surmised by Wolfram Fischer, industrialisation began in Germany even 'before the great spurt in the mid-nineteenth century; and although it is something that is not so visible statistically, it was, in essence, a process that contained all the later germs of development'. In short, it is problematic whether the industrial revolution in France and Germany was not quite different to the case of England, as David S. Landes supposes.

Ths historian is confronted by similar problems when he tries to use Kondratieff's 'long cycles', theory to systematically structure historical tradition. As the 'long cycles', as 'bridges of observed continuity are applied to the general succession of events' (E. Wagemann), the difficulties already observed in relation to the theory of the stages of economic growth re-emerge: namely, the interpretation of qualitative material by quantitative methods. In addition, there is a second problem connected with the theory of business cycles involving a degree of uncertainty in the calculation of both the basic cycle and the regularity of the swings. The method devised by Kondratieff for eliminating the trend (the least-square method) was criticised at an early date, and it was emphasised that the very opposite could be proved by the same method. The result, according to Finck von Finckenstein, was 'a process equally complex and complicated as the time sequence itself'. But that is not all. Because Kondratieff and his successors had failed to define the prerequisites of their trend comparisons, their calculations were classified by trade cycle theorists and mathematicians as 'arbitrary' (O. Anderson). With the relatively short observation period of $2\frac{1}{2}$ cycles, 'the nature of the model to be applied inevitably implies a trend hypothesis, and as a result the preconditions for its calculation eliminate the proof of long cycles right from the beginning' (U. Weinstock).

In the face of such uncertainty in the model and the confusing number of calculated trend variations of the trade cycles, one must ask if the historian has the right to use for his own ends the pattern of trend periods as '. . . a satisfactory and uniform principle of periodisation which fits in with the long-term fluctuating dynamic of the development of the whole economy' (H. Rosenberg). It is also questionable whether Knut Borchardt is right in regarding this model as one of the few offers from the warehouse of economic theory which the historian can take over or simply acquire.

Until now, the scepticism of German historians towards theory in general has been very strong, largely because of tradition. The German historian has tended to follow what has been handed down, and has arranged newly-won knowledge within the framework of what has already been acquired. This has also been the case in economic and social history. Apart from the research work in agrarian history, where Wilhelm Abel in particular has tried to determine the long swings as 'fundamental units of time', it cannot be denied that as a means of helping to define epochs, long-term trends in the trade cycle have remained largely ignored in those works on German economic and social history which have so far appeared. The works of Spiethoff and Schumpeter have found no response. Instead, the political cut-off points of national, state and political developments have frequently been regarded as the natural determining dates even for changes in the economic and social sphere, and have been interpreted as such. Theories apparently have not been brought into play. Attempts to assess economic development have frequently been exhausted in the enumeration of facts, or in endeavours to portray the individual sectors of economic and social change at best in an isolated fashion and with the help of philologically descriptive methods.

As a result, one of the most important preconditions for an adequate interpretation of these problems has been lost, as only the recognition of the interdependence of political and economic forces can result in a critical presentation of the problems involved. Although it is imperative, for example, to adopt a systematic approach to historical research in order to be able to represent human activity in its transmitted form, equally it is impossible to ignore the time-factors, as all theories do. Similarly, the attempt to comprehend political and economic structures only appears sensible to the historian from the point of view of a temporal chronology, which cannot be made up or regarded in an experimental light. This means that an economic and social history can neither afford to start from *a priori* fixed models which only seek in extant historical material the proof for the theory, nor can it be a simple list or association of dates. And it is in this context that the theory of the stages of growth, as well as that of the 'long cycles', proves of importance to the historian in the critical assessment of the past, as far as this is possible from state and private archives, memoirs, newspapers, magazines, business reports, statistical tables and not least, contemporary publications.

In the first place the historian must inquire into the facts and use these as a starting point. He cannot be satisfied with a presentation of a fascinating and synchronised version of economic and political development, when the theories of the 'long cycles' upon which the synchronisation depends can present different sequences of phases according to each separate theoretical explanation. He cannot, therefore, satisfy himself with a rational assessment to provide a basis for regarding the long-term trend periods as 'units that provide a structured form and integration' for historical development (J. Schumpeter). He will nevertheless be able, with the help of these rationalised concepts, to form an effective judgement of the past and of a substantial feature of economic development, namely the trend and above all the lag between different trends. Although it has often been surmised in this connection that the oscillations around the trend can only be used for interpretative purposes to a far lesser degree than theoretical considerations demand, the business cycle and growth theories can provide a structured framework for a representation of German economic and social history. But this framework must inevitably be integrated with the contemporary scene of social events. No single theory, however, can provide the sort of framework into which individual historical facts can simply be fitted. Indeed, it is most important to establish break-off points on the basis of a widely-held argument and with reference to source materials, not in order to support a previously calculated theory, but far more pragmatically, with the purpose of doing justice to the nature of historical events. The historian will benefit from the research results of the statistical and theoretical aspects of economics without having to surrender to a dependence on mechanistic principles of thought. With the help of the trend cycles, for example, the years 1873 to 1896 can be understood as a unified period, although the cycle theory cannot provide an explanation for the politically and economically decisive events of the year 1879. A similar relationship exists in the case of the economic crisis of 1857 which also fails to fit into the pattern of the calculated business cycle curve from 1847 to 1873. And finally, the doubt concerning the international nature and generality of the long-wave business cycle cannot be dismissed, if a comparison is made between English and German industrial development in the period between 1896 and 1913. The English economy in fact stagnated during this imperialistic upswing of the Kondratieff cycle.

We have thus returned to the starting-point of our deliberations: the comparability of the industrial changes in individual countries and the characterisation of Germany at the turn of the eighteenth century as an underdeveloped area. If one accepts the basic approach of the stages of growth theory, namely the essentially uniform progress of industrial growth without attention to national, social and political preconditions, then the uncritical comparison with England would be justified, as would the preceding portrayal of the economic situation of Germany. but can one accept this approach?

The German territories and their policies had a different tradition from that of England; and without due attention to the root conditions of their state identity, which is to be found in enlightened despotism, neither the economic, social and political situation of Germany at the turn of the eighteenth century, nor the 'administered' economy of the German territories can be fully understood. If the situation is examined in detail, the German territories were not underdeveloped, but had developed differently. Indeed, in certain areas of civil organisation they were so far developed that the radical industrial and social changes taking place in Western Europe failed to have an immediate and direct effect in these regions. The discrepancy between tradition and emancipation was often over-exaggerated by enlightened despotism (W. Conze). According to R. Stadelmann,

> ... Germany had not participated in the threefold development which England, the United States of America and France had undergone in a carefully delineated rhythm and gradually increasing tempo – the step from an absolute state to a democratic and representative constitution; the opportune transition from feudalism to a social order based on equality; and the development of a concept of state citizenship in place of the traditional hierarchical order.

The demands of the French Revolution for liberty, equality and fraternity had certainly been heard east of the Rhine, but they had found just as few supporters as the English concept of a chamber of representatives with a responsible cabinet, an interchange of coalitions capable of forming a government and a state judiciary which was supposed to punish infringements of the constitution. The reasons for the immunity of the German territories to these movements and ideas are numerous and varied and cannot be discussed here. However, one phenomenon which can be regarded as important must be stressed. Germany experienced the Englightenment only in the form of absolutism, and this was to have important consequences.

It was principally due to enlightened despotism that the spark of 1789 did not catch fire in Germany. As convinced supporters of governmental reform, the third estate in the German territories wanted nothing to do with a radical conflict with the nobility and the church. What was wanted, keeping in mind the princely attempts to remove the crassest abuses of the old order, was a princely state founded in law, where the government was concerned with securing employment possibilities, keeping the priests in their place, drying out the swamps, building primary schools and caring for the poor. The government's role was to protect the poor against the rich, the peasants against the nobility and the diligent citizens against the

14

claimants of hereditary rights. What was really wanted, in effect, was a bureaucratic state where everything was to be dealt with 'reasonably', and not on the basis of corruption (R. Stadelmann). According to the opinion of those citizens connected by privilege with the nobility, particularly the upper classes, the military, ecclesiastics, teachers, administrative officials, doctors and academics, 'Revolutions were completely out of the question as long as governments were continuously just and continuously awake and met demands with opportune improvements, and did not resist too long until the bare essentials had to be forced through from below' (Goethe).

Certainly the initial shadows cast by the 'social question' were recognised, and it was realised that if a solution to this question was not found, the unity of state and society would dissolve 'in so far as the *societas civilis* no longer corresponded to the structure of formalised Estates' (R. Kosellek). But it was believed, on the other hand, that the question could be solved in terms of the traditional unity of state and society, rather than by radical means. The upsurges of the French Revolution and its outrages, as they were regarded, 'were too close for comfort and every day and every hour gave rise to shock, whereas its beneficial results ... were not to be seen'. In contrast, the attempts of the princes and their administrative officials – who had begun to encourage investments, not only in the public but also in the private sector – were already recognisable. Despite the fact that the unusually high population growth-rate which became evident towards the end of the eighteenth century prevented an effective increase in total production, and despite the extended growth of pre-industrial mass poverty and the fall in average levels of consumption, the relatively strong revival of economic activity, the attempted reforms of the customs system and the timorous inception of the emancipation of the peasantry initiated by state legislation all contributed to the fact that peace and order reigned in the German territories. Even without the increase in *per capita* net social product, government reform attempts were accepted as proof of the beneficent disposition of the princes and as the successful beginning of more comprehensive reforms. What had been extorted in France by a bloody revolution and in England by new organisations and techniques, in short through the machine, could be obtained in Germany, it was hoped, and certainly with some justification, by means of reconciliation between the monarchy and the Estates. The dismantling of the traditional rights of individual estates was designed to introduce on a gradual basis a constitutional change, which was to provide the framework for an economically free society which was nevertheless still incorporated within the state. The 'draft for a new society' (R. Kosellek) was not intended to result in the abolition of all aristocratic rights, but only those which prevented the 'opening up of a genuine economic sphere of activity'. In the words of the Prussian King Frederick II, 'Skilful merchants, manufacturers and artists are of more use to the state than the complete corps of present lawyers.'

2

Preparatory steps:
the Agricultural Revolution

Prior to 1806 the nobility had a secured position, the middle classes were defined by privileges, and the peasantry, both free and servile, was dependent and knew its place. Personal freedom was seen in terms of state ties and its usefulness to the state and the existing order. The exclusiveness of the nobility was not questioned. Admittedly, towards the end of the eigtheenth century there has been a slow change in economic conditions, with a transition to crop rotation and a more intensive form of livestock farming. This had been accompanied by an increasing indebtedness of estate and landholders, which had intensified changes in property-holding and had induced a hesitant official policy of reform in the sphere of customs policy and agriculture. Nevertheless, the nobility was still in a position to retain its political and social power and pre-eminence.

Although this era frequently witnessed dismal mass poverty in the cities and rural areas, it was a time marked by a timid start to reform, by the brilliance of late baroque development and by bourgeois aristocratic spirituality. A whole world collapsed with the arrival of Napoleon's soldiers, for whom the German traditions, privileges and corporative organisations had no significance. Although it was possible to shake off the Napoleonic occupation and

17

dominance after twenty years, the reactionary princely administrations were no longer able to reassume their previous rights in the liberated territories. Despite the brilliant restoration of the principle of legitimacy, despite the Holy Alliance, Christian and conservative policies, the ubiquitous censorship of the Metternich school and a reactionary policy of police control, the conflict with the new powers and ideas – primarily with the problems of the 'Nation', the 'Constitution' and the 'Machine' – had now become unavoidable for the German princely houses.

Already during the period of occupation it had become clear that the *res publica sive societas civilis*[1] in the traditional German form, particularly in Prussia, was incapable of dealing with the problem of the indebtedness of the German territories in general and of the agricultural estates in particular. It was equally incapable of raising the demanded contributions and completely powerless to avoid the catastrophic consequences of the Continental blockade. In East Prussia grain prices fell by 60 to 80% and shipping traffic by roughly 60%. The silk trade of Berlin and the Silesian linen and Brandenburg cloth trade, which constituted 50% of total Prussian exports, lost their foreign markets (W. Treue). But it was not only the basis of the Prussian economy that was shaken by these developments. If the very foundation of the political order were not to be endangered or even to be drawn into the whirlpool of revolutionary upheaval, it was necessary, according to the views of the reformers in the new administrations, to find a solution with a 'legal basis, with prudent regulations, unity and authority'. Reforms had become necessary. A start was accordingly made with 'decreed reforms' in the traditional mould, 'with the intention of establishing a new society of citizens, progressing from top to bottom and from a central core outwards'. This new society was also 'to be capable of raising the cash demanded' (R. Kosellek).

The administrative authorities, which had already been partly reorganised during the period of the Napoleonic

---

1. 'The State or the fellowship of citizens'.

Imperium and were now separated from the judiciary, hoped to be able to utilise the economic resources of the enlarged territories more effectively, by releasing economic potential, by the emancipation of the peasantry and by the introduction of freedom of trade and new urban regulations. By these means financial demands could also be met. In the first instance they were concerned with the abolition of the legal rights protecting property-holding and landlordism and the protective wall of guild privileges, with the purpose of creating freedom of work which was essentially designed to be a freedom to pay contribution assessments. At the same time, this legislation was intended to establish, by the indirect means of reform, a 'sensible class order' and a new state organisation, without completely dissolving the old order, which was largely dependent on the property-owning connection. The intention was to create new links with property by means of 'emancipation' and the freeing of economic resources. This would ensure not only the formation of a new and solvent state apparatus, but also the preservation of inherited rights and handed-down traditions. With reforms based on the model of estate and municipal systems of a largely old Germanic pattern, but also incorporating in part English and French examples, the reorganisation of the German territories was designed to lead to the reshaping of the German Empire as a Christian and educative power.

The most important precondition for the plan of political education, which stemmed from the financial crisis, was, as already stated, the provision of personal freedom. In this respect the consequent dismantling of those rights which had hitherto prevented the release of individual initiative was begun, but at a rate and to an extent which varied enormously from one territory to another. The traditional element of paternal authority within German society was reduced in a relatively short time, by means of laws on peasant emancipation, freedom of trade and the introduction of new urban regulations. The process involved the implementation of a new state law, a new law of contract, the reorganisation of the school education system and the separation and restructuring of the judiciary and executive. The rapidity of the transition was particularly noticeable in Prussia. The importance of the family was now limited and the mobilisation of the lower classes provided the basis for a division of productive capacity, the extension of industry and the transition from a natural to a cash economy. At the same time attempts were made to encourage 'the art of organisation' and work discipline. As it appeared feasible to 'impose' the 'interpenetration of man with a spirit of industriousness', the problem of achieving a 'technical and physical culture' was entrusted to the 'universally inspiring force of the administration'.

The confidence of the reformers in the spirit of the times soon proved to be illusory. Although the 'nation's experts' (B. Hildebrand) were indeed able to break down the barrier of the estates and to release the 'strongest pent-up potential of economically employable entrepreneurial forces' (C. Jantke), the attempted fusion of these liberated forces with the state and their chaining to the administration was not successful. The prerogatives of the estates could not be abolished, nor the opposition of the nobility overcome. The liberal advance initiated by the reformers therefore remained ambivalent and was indeed destined to continue as such, as both the conditions under which the reforms had been undertaken, as well as their aims, precluded the existence of any uniform policy.

In particular the course of peasant emancipation shows the dilemma in which the reformers found themselves, and the double-edged nature of their measures. Although it had been begun with the intention of winning the support of the lower classes for a free economic order and to make possible their acquisition of property and political responsibility, in the final analysis it led much less to the emergence of responsibility among the peasantry and their absorption into the state through property ownership, than to a renewed reinforcement of the estate position of the nobility and of land- and estate-holders at the direct expense of the peasantry. Without any doubt the landlords were those who gained from the central European process of farm consolidation. By means of land secession, purchase, and forceful eviction, the estate owners in East Germany gained almost a million hectares[2] of cultivable land and thereby created a first prerequisite for a market-orientated system of large-scale production geared to the needs of industry. But even more important for the 'profound restructuring of the social and economic order' (F. Lütge) was the abolition of traditional servile and tithe connections, the lifting of restrictions on the division of land, inheritance and mortgage commitments, the redistribution of cultivable land, the consolidation of field strips, the abolition of the commons, and finally the transformation along liberal lines of the old conditions of work. These changes provided the basis for the rationalisation of the whole work process, both in the sphere of seigneurial lordship and in estate ownership. At the same time emancipation benefited the peasant through the disappearance of numerous obligations and services, but this development also constituted an equal emancipation for the landlords. The paternal lord no longer had to care for the free citizens of the state, and he was as much rid of his duties and obligations as the peasant. He was therefore able to utilise his financial potential, his entrepreneurial ability and his estate prerogatives in the interest of improving and extending his properties. As the nobility had been assured of a guarantee of ownership, the enjoyment of traditional local authority and the continuation of the existing system of land taxation prior to each act of abolition and regulation, it was able not only to retain its traditional leading position in the state, but also to strengthen this quite appreciably. The tendency was reinforced in the eastern parts of Germany, where the nobility continued to unite in its hands the rights of patronage, local police and the judiciary. The abolition of the corporative order in rural areas was followed not only by the release of an army of unqualified workers from the land and the destruction of the peasantry as a dependent but highly entitled estate, but also by the realignment of regional

2. 1 hectare = 10,000 sq. metres.

groupings of authority along the lines of a new professional class. It proved just as difficult for the administration to achieve the integration of this new professional class in the new state, as the provision for, assimilation and absorption of those who had previously lived in service and in a protected milieu.

The Continental system and the agrarian crisis of the 1820s played a significant role in this context. They effectively prevented the realisation of the goal of the reforms, namely that the freed peasant would be able to pay his debts and receive a fair price and adequate return for his work on the inferior arable land and poorly utilisable pasture to which he had been forced by the Emancipation. The nobility and the estate-holders could, despite a marketing and liquidity crisis and frequent changes in the ownership of property, retain and even extend their economic and political position; yet the freed peasant, who was heavily indebted, lost the basis of his existence through the lifting of indebtedness restrictions. He was compelled to seek his living, initially as a free rural labourer, then as an allowance worker and finally as a seasonal worker with short-term work contracts. And as the regulated and rationalised system of large-scale farming – which remained at the same time liable to crises – failed to provide employment opportunities either for the freed peasant or for his numerous children, both the peasant class and those engaged partly in agriculture and partly in rural trades (as well as the rural proletariat) were forced to emigrate. The problem was compounded by the fact that after 1815 the rural population increased by over 50% in a few years, in a period when provisions for the poor were no longer being made by the landowning class. Propertyless, uprooted, homeless, belonging neither to the state nor an estate, almost half the inhabitants of the German territories lived in poverty and misery.

This meant that the result of the revolution in agriculture and the abolition of personal dependence, without the complete removal of estate privileges, was not only an extension of the cultivable area (which has been roman-tically glorified in the intervening period), the regulation of land distribution as a prerequisite for the economic competitiveness of a rural estate economy, and freedom of movement and the release of new labour potential, but also the 'mass poverty of those directly dependent on the state'. As the antithesis between poor and rich was no longer forcibly contained within the framework of the family and the household, it burst open. Newly-forming classes were conscious of their plight and the hopelessness of their economic position.

A similar development took place in the realm of trade and industry. As in the case of agriculture the state administration was unable to prevent in this instance the fact that measures originally designed to strengthen the predominance of the state bureaucracy and administration and the activation of underprivileged social groups eventually produced the opposite effect. The abolition of guild privileges and traditional trading rights, the state-initiated attempt to inculcate an 'industrious consciousness', the ending of the state's role as a guardian of economic enterprise and the ordained activation of a system of free competition – all these reforms finally failed due to the successful opposition of the craftsmen. This group represented the traditional forces in society, which received support not only from the conservative nobility, but also from the educated bourgeoisie concerned over the increasing destitution of the familes of craftsmen, and from sections of the bureaucracy. It quickly became clear that, despite the successful abolition of supervised and privileged trade regulations in this sector, this enactment did not lead to or only inadequately facilitated the integration of the individual in the mechanism of the decreed free market economy – prepared by means of legislation, administrative measures and state entrepreneurial activity. Such an integration could have taken place only if the freeing of new resources in the secondary sector had been accompanied by an extension in production, and if a general advance could have been achieved with the help of the new organisations and techniques promoted by the bureaucratic institutions of the state. This advance, however, failed to materialise. The volume of transport in the German territories stagnated, and only in 1835 was the living standard of 1805 regained.

Indebtedness, the Continental blockade and the agrarian crisis also severely affected industrial development. In particular, the consequences of the Continental blockade had a serious impact on this sector. After the lifting of the blockade. The stockpiled English goods streamed over the Continent and ruined the incipient growth of the young, but under-capitalised, German industry which had emerged during the blockade in order to supply substitute goods.[3] It now became apparent that although Germany had a relatively developed industrial sector in comparison with its eastern neighbours, the gulf between English and Continental industrial development had become still wider during the years of Bonapartist imperialism. The shipping industry and commerce were ruined. Markets were as meagre as they had been before, and primarily served purely local needs. Capital, despite all the efforts of the bureaucracy to promote industrial growth, continued to be invested in state and agricultural loans. There was a shortage of the banks that could have financed the desired innovations and could have adjusted the distribution of capital to match, for example, the new customs policy initiated by Prussia. The traditional organisation of industrial production continued to set the tone, even after considerable extensions in the market had been achieved through the Customs Union. Just as before, the predominant organisational unit remained the family concern, which was often endangered by crises and which offered no possibility of expansion. The concept of the family continued to determine the limits of the concern and thereby precluded any innovation. There was no basic lack of entrepreneurial possibilities and enterprise, yet the reformatory efforts of the 'technological organisers' such as Beuth, Kunth and Steinbeis[4] had no success worth men-

3. R. H. Tilly, 'Los von England: Probleme des Nationalismus in der deutschen Wirtschaftsgeschichte', in *Zeitschrift für die gesamte Staatswissenschaft*. Vol. 124, Tübingen: 1968.
4. See Appendix for biographies of these industrialists.

tioning within the Customs Union. Their initiatives were thwarted both by the crises of the primary sector, which were 'of decisive importance for the further development of economic and social reforms' (C. Jantke) and by the intellectual and economic immobility of the practitioners of traditional crafts. Technical ignorance was accompanied by the impossibility of organisational development, and the guild attitude went hand in hand with the politics of self-interest practised by the restoration nobility. The German textile industry, widely scattered in the Rhineland, in Saxony, Silesia, Bavaria and Württemberg, consisted entirely of small craft and family concerns. No new spinning machine was introduced into Germany before 1840. The production technique remained traditional and centred in rural areas, despite continuously sinking prices and starvation wages. In certain areas, for example in Saxony, the number of spindles actually declined and in the unprotected German cotton industry the initiative of entrepreneurs after 1840 remained devoid of success until after 1850. The same picture can be found in the woollen industry. There was little demand in any case for this luxury product from among the largely poor population. The marketing possibilities were extra-ordinarily slight, and growth in this sector of industry was accordingly slow. In addition, German articles were poor and could not compete in quality with French, Belgian or even English goods. Both 'scientific knowledge and educated taste' (Kunth) were lacking.

The situation in the iron industry was not much better. New and independent innovations were also lacking in this sector and such extension and industrial development as there was, followed the lines of the traditional system of organisation. There were very few technical changes. Wood, water and wind, as the old sources of energy, remained in the first instance the basis of the industry. Coal was used only when it could be obtained in the vicinity of river transport. The substitution of iron for wood, and introduction of the machine for organic power, was not customary prior to 1840, despite the efforts of such individuals as Fr. Harkort, Fr. Krupp, Egells, Borsig, Eges-torff, Schichau, Maffei and Jacob Mayer.[5]

In the heavy industry sector, which is more capital-intensive in terms of equipment and fixtures than the textile industry, the deficiencies in the circulation of capital had a particularly disadvantageous effect. As heavy industry, together with the textile industry, provided the catalyst for industrial growth, development in the years 1830–40 was very slow. Well into the 1850s, the western areas of Germany had no iron works which depended on coke. Although the state-run mines and iron works of Upper Silesia had at their disposal quite good technical equipment, their productivity growth rates, except in one or two special cases, remained minimal. And yet a demand existed. Belgium, which acted as the catalyst for German industrial development, financed its own industrial upswing on the basis of German demand.

Commensurate with the extremely slow rate of technical development and organisational restructuring of industry, the application of new sources of energy was equally delayed. Ignorance and fear of the dangers of machines were as significant in this respect as the absence of the need to replace the power supplied by horses, water, wind and human labour. The chemical industry found itself in a similar situation: general living standards and productive capacity were not sufficient to create a profitable demand for soap, dyes and glass goods.

Despite the intensive efforts of the administration to revive business with the help of technical universities, polytechnic schools, craft institutes and model state concerns, and by making machines and loans available, the reorganisation of this sector of the economy remained stillborn. On the other hand, the decreed freedom of trade and industry, the liberalisation of customs policies and the general economic policy of creating large customs areas and therefore more efficient markets, had produced a decline in craft production. It was this aspect which was most significant for contemporaries. With the destruction

5. See Appendix for biographies.

of the guilds the production unit of the master craftsman was depressed to the poverty level of a one-man concern. This newly emergent class was incapable of competing with machine-produced articles from England. They were not in a position to pay taxes and were forced, together with their women and children, to make their own living. They saw the cause of their misery in the reform policies of the governments, and in particular in the liberal customs policies forced through by Prussia. They therefore focussed their efforts on securing the reintroduction of the old guild order and customs duties. Demands for the restoration of these institutions were increasing, and they became identified with the interests of the nobility in their opposition to the administration.

But this was not all. The limitations on the number of journeymen and apprentices and the abolition of the production methods allowed by the guilds, had resulted in the freeing of non-maintained workers, who increased the army of the unemployed and the poor. The administration failed to bind this social group to the new state. But, in contrast to the paupers on the land, this growing class did not accept its fate without opposition. To an increasing extent it served to catalyse a revolutionary movement, whose leaders demanded a radical realignment in the distribution of property and the division of state authority.

Thus the administration became isolated, represented as it was by a small upper layer of officials, distinguished by their humanistic education, a thorough training in cameralist and legal studies and by property. The traditional social structure, which was to have been revived and made more effective by means of reforms, began to disintegrate. A similar process also began to affect the narrow union between the state, society and the economy, which was not to have been disturbed by the reforms, but improved and reanimated. One factor contributing to this development was the restoration of the nobility, the opposition of the craft workers and the emancipation of the poor and propertyless as a new social class. Another factor of equal importance was the continuously increasing rate of growth in production from the 1840s onwards, accompanied by the extension of the factory system and the use of machine power. Of crucial importance, however, was the increase and acceleration in the volume of transport and foreign trade, which resulted from the policy of state support in the context of a planned economy, the construction of roads and railways, the regulation of canal and river traffic and finally the English demand for cereals. It now became evident that the new leaders of industrial concerns could not be 'bound'. They did not regard the state's preparatory work and previous achievements, which had led to the breakthrough of bourgeois doctrine, as something positive that had been realised by the system of bureaucratic government.

To an increasing degree, opposition stemmed from both the reactionary agrarian, feudal and guild elements of the restoration, and from the proponents of the technical, liberal advance, as well as the impoverished rural and urban workers. They turned increasingly against the proposed policy of a synthesis between mercantilism and liberalism, as put forward by the bureaucracy. They also opposed a pre-ordained and regulated economic freedom, which to one side appeared too free and to the other side too restricted, and which was therefore denounced by all groups concerned. However, the unity of state and society, which was the intended aim of the administration, was not strictly rejected by the majority of opponents. A solution to the tension increasingly evident between rich and poor and between agriculture and industry did appear to exist in the reconciliation between the monarchy and the estates, between policies that had already proved their worth and those of a more modern type, and in timely improvements from above. But the conflicts between the bureaucracy and the newly developing classes became more acute in the 1840s in the wake of secular economic growth. It became increasingly apparent that the period of stagnation in the process of economic development had been overcome and that the multiplier effect (H. Rosenberg) of railway construction had precipitated a hesitant revival of the economy, which therefore led to a certain prosperity, particularly among the established middle classes. But the more feasible it became to formulate political demands on the basis of economic advancement, the more apparent it became that, despite the radical reorganisation of property, income and conditions relating to landholding, population structure and class during the first third of the nineteenth century, the old power-holding cliques had not been superseded. The land-holding nobility, just as before, continued to determine the criteria by which political influence and social power were measured. They had also seen to it that, with the restoration of the guild organisation and the tightening-up of regulations governing social class, settlement and marriage, economic freedom had not been realised too quickly. The manufacturers, bankers, academics and the majority of the population from those sectors of society below the level of the defined estates (namely the proletariat) continued to be denied any form of political participation. The interest groups representing industry could find representation only in the reactivated estate society 'when they appeared as the representatives of landed property' (R. Kosellek) by adapting themselves to the old German tradition.

By means of an economic policy interwoven both with restorative class elements and educative, liberal aspects, which had its basis in an unnatural and forced partnership between enlightened reformers in the administration and traditionalists among the aristocracy, traditions were both continued and refounded. These were to have a decisive importance in all the later phases of political and economic history, even within the framework of the nation state. In this symbiosis, which was renewed after the abortive attempt at revolutionary change in 1848, the antithesis between a traditional social order and a levelled mass society, as well as the problem of the delayed decorporisation (W. Conze) of the German state and social structure, was as prominent as the tendency towards the preservation of historical continuity in a world undergoing revolutionary change through the pressure of industrial development. A common trend throughout this period was the continued obedience towards authority and the trust shown by even the majority of the working class in the state and its administration. In addition, class antagonisms were restructured on the basis of an administrative and constructive solution. The eastern provinces were increasingly stripped of all trade and industry. Deurbanisation took place in the East, aggravating the tension between East and West, between agriculture and industry. In short, the structural cleavage of Germany, with all its consequences, was just as widespread in the years of the *Vormärz*[6] as the antagonisms in the constitutional, political, economic and social spheres between the authorities and the subject and between the reactivated estate order and those without any social position who now constituted an emergent class.

In 1840 Liebig's standard work *Die organische Chemie in ihrer Anwendung auf Agrikultur und Physiologie*[7] had appeared, and just prior to this the agricultural teachings of Thaer, Schubarth, Gentz, Krugs, Koppe and Schönleithner,[8] together with Thünen's treatise *Isolierter Staat in Beziehung auf Landwirtschaft und Nationalökonomie*,[9] had prepared the way for the emergence of an agricultural system suitable for a highly capitalised industrial state. But despite all the restructuring of agricultural activity on an economic and technical basis, despite all the diversification of the traditional seigneurial and corporative order, the ideology of the unity of state and society and the concept of the 'whole house' remained alive in central Europe and proved so resistant to all the democratic and constitutional tendencies associated with emergent industrialisation that not only did it facilitate the restoration of the political predominance of the nobility, but also an alliance of the protagonists of industrial advancement with the feudal world of the Estates.

6. The *Vormärz* is an expression commonly used to denote the period 1815–48.
7. J. v. Liebig, *Chemistry in its Application to Agriculture and Physiology*.
8. See Appendix for biographies.
9. J. H. von Thünen, *The Isolated State*, 1826. Modern English translation by C. W. Wartenberg, edited with an introduction by P. Hall, Oxford: 1966. See Appendix for his bibliography.

Preparation for the Agricultural Revolution

The events of 1848, then, brought to light the tensions which had built up during the thirty years following the rule of Napoleon, and showed how ambivalent progress had in fact been. The solution of these tensions made equally clear the significance of the state-initiated industrial and agricultural upswing for German development in general. Although that development cannot be measured statistically in detail, a start had been made. Contributory factors included the emancipation of the peasantry, freedom of trade and industry, the revision of municipal statutes and the creation of trading states enclosing large geographical areas. At a later date, with the creation of the Customs Union, with railway construction and policies relating to roads, schooling and trade, these developments – once policitical and social tensions had been resolved – would lead to an economic community of interest between, on the one hand, merchants, bankers and industrialists, and on the other hand, the leading members of the feudal and conservative agricultural sector.

Although the year of the 'German Revolution' did not mark any clear break in the pattern of German economic development, from the point of view of the general trend, the events of that year were of epoch-making significance in German economic and social history. Henceforth, the administration no longer held the active leadership in economic matters, and its role was taken over by private entrepreneurs. In an extremely short space of time, in a great spurt of only a few years, it proved possible to secure the integration and competitiveness of German production in the world markets, although the gap between Germany and England still remained. One of the most important prerequisites for this upswing was the official acceptance of institutions which were able to direct capital accumulation and the strategy of concerns in the new industrial sector. The banks were also able to unite the dispersed resources and put them to a better use. Regarded in this light, the refounding of the Schaaffhausen bank as a joint-stock company, which was the first act of the revolutionary ministry of Hansemann and Camphausen, was the starting signal for the take-off in Germany.

3

The Great Spurt:
Imported Progress

Supported by the educated middle class, the majority of representatives in the national assembly at Frankfurt in 1848 had been concerned 'with acting in the interest of protecting the whole German fatherland and the throne'. It was the general intention of the assembly, in the words of its president, 'to build an assembly that would desire freedom'. But it was also to continue 'to adhere to the monarchy' and 'to our princely houses', as Dahlmann stated in his preface to the new constitutional reform. 'The old habit of obedience was tied to these institutions and could not easily be transferred at will anywhere else'. This majority did not, on any account, want revolution, radicalism, full sovereignty of the people, or equality of all political rights. Despite the initial and violent unloading of pent-up tensions, which had their origin as much in economic distress as in the constitutional promises which had never been honoured, the tradition of obedience towards authority was not broken. Indeed, it came to influence the movement in an increasingly positive way, the more the 'revolution' became entangled in the insoluable antithesis which emerged with elemental force in the three main problems faced by the national assembly. The first problem concerned the national state and its boundaries, or, to be precise, its relationship to Denmark, Poland and the

32

national movements in Austria. The second problem concerned the form of the state and the constitution. In other words, would it be possible to placate the old forces? And finally, there was the problem of economic and social legislation, to deal with the contemporary economic emergency.

In the course of the conflicts of the summer of 1848, it became apparent that the reform legislation had not only removed the cause for the revolutionary uprising, but already contained the conditions for the apparent solution of the existing antitheses. The majority of revolutionary leaders did not want to destroy the basis of the state, nor the feudal aristocracy dependent on landed property, nor the army. They saw that their own interests would be preserved through an arrangement with these forces. As a result, the future development of Germany was decided.

Those citizens supporting national and liberal ideals were disturbed by the revolts against the fiscal authorities, the castle, the manufacturer's villa and the machine shop. They were equally tired of what one contemporary described as the 'soldiers' game' played out in the 'phrases, newspapers and babbling of the people's tribunes'. They were alarmed by the ruin of credit and the increasing economic misery. These citizens therefore sought protection and refuge in the state administration, and finally opted for princely calm and order. They were convinced that 'the lower classes of society as such could never constitute a lasting power in the state' and that their power 'could only be a transitory one as an instrument of a more astute political party'. Caught between social revolution and the protection of private property, between unity and freedom, a republic or a monarchy, the restoration of order became a question of the reorganisation of credit and the granting of constitutional rights as far as the spokesmen of those citizens involved in the economy as well as in politics were concerned.

In this way, after all the reasonable demands had been granted amazingly quickly, the reformers, entrepreneurs and members of the propertied class united with the old order in the hope of continuing to play a determining role

in an alliance with the landholders and nobility. A manufacturer from Barmen observed towards the end of 1848
that 'what yesterday had still been liberal, was today conservative' and that 'the former conservatives were only too
willing to join forces with today's free-thinkers'. They
were satisfied with the constitution which had already
been achieved, or at least promised, in view of the existence of social and revolutionary radicalism. This was
made considerably easier because, on the economic level,
a whole row of concessions had been extorted, which were
of more importance to the merchants, bankers and entrepreneurs than any political advance. The newly-found
community of interest between the feudal aristocracy, the
army and the patricians of title and money had been
instrumental in this respect. It also probably became
apparent that the disposition for reform had been very
quickly forgotten once the decision was made to opt for the
'old state'. The attempt to make the urban middle class into
the new pillars of the state could not succeed. Equally, it
was impossible to prize the nobility away from its military
and feudal base and, by means of a bourgeois parliamentary system, to reconcile them to the social and
economic developments of the century. The reconciliation
had proved illusory. But in the field of economic legislation and matters pertaining to the constitution so much
had in any case been achieved to allow the ordinary citizen
a possibility, even if this possibility were a very limited
one, of political action in a traditional German sense. The
majority of people in 1848 had, in any case, never aspired
to anything beyond such a form of co-operation. There
was, indeed, disappointment over the increasingly obvi-
ous lack of success in relation to particular political pro-
grammes and the fact that there had been almost no
attempt to oppose the restoration of the old authorities.
They felt themselves compensated, however, in the
economic sphere; and their whole energy and initiative
was channelled into the further development of industry,
with the purpose of achieving the political unity of the
nation and thereby the freedom which would then inevitably follow.

As a result, the political situation in Germany after 1848 was marked by a renewed coalition between the old and the new forces and one which was marked, if one can express it in this way, by a division of labour between the nobility, property-holders and the middle classes. The dominant groups in the economy recognised the traditional leading role of the nobility, property-holders and the administration in the political field, which in turn allowed the entrepreneurs to manage their affairs as they liked. At the same time it tried to make provision for the middle class in rural areas and for traditional crafts threatened by industrialisation. In this way the nobility once again secured its own position, while the middle class was able to extend its economic role, without the administration acting as a guardian. It therefore believed itself to be protected from the 'fourth estate'. The industrial revolution and the fear of its main product – the social question – therefore became the motive power behind development.

Probably the most tangible effect of the German revolution was the strengthening of monarchical and feudal power and the weakening of the authority of the administration, which had previously been excessively powerful. At the same time the revolution defused the social and revolutionary claims of the proletariat and satisfied the bourgeoisie in its search for success through the promotion of a capitalist economy, despite the fact that the extent to which this had been undertaken varied substantially from one individual state to another. This development took place in a period characterised by a stormy upswing and a desultory increase in productivity, particularly in the iron and coal industries. It had been carried forward by a soaring boom in an agricultural sector unaffected by any recession, particularly in those areas east of the Elbe. The state of agriculture had been transformed by reforms, improvements in agricultural techniques, crop rotation, the forced extension of arable cultivation and vastly increased holdings of livestock. All these factors contributed to high yields at a time of continuously rising prices and good marketing conditions, particularly in trade with England. Now, in addition, the initial reforms and the technological projects of the 1820s and '30s began to bear fruit in the industrial sector in the years after 1850. The market organisations and foreign trading connections which had been formed in the 1830s now proved their usefulness. Consumer needs were awakened, note-issuing banks were founded and private banks formed themselves into consortia which were designed to serve the needs of industry to a far greater extent than those of the agricultural sector or the state. In Prussia, investments in industry began to overtake those in the public sector, and foreign capital – which had previously held back and indeed had not been required – now found its way into Germany, particularly into the western provinces of Prussia.

The founding of the first German banks was an expression of the extent to which the Customs Union had participated in the economic boom between 1850 and 1857. It was part of an economic process of international dimensions, which prompted the reduction of the English grain duties in 1846, activated railway construction in America and Europe and hastened the outbreak of the Crimean War. A number of factors had also produced an increase and acceleration in the volume of transport. This development had been facilitated by the construction of an integrated European traffic system, which had been begun in the 1840s, and by the first significant increase in ship capacity and a corresponding expansion of shipping lines, particularly to South America. Ancillary factors included the extension in the network of turnpike roads and the regulation of European waterways. Demand for coal, raw cotton and iron rose. Connected with this was the construction of factory installations, living accommodation and settlements. New production centres which quickly altered the face of the German landscape emerged. The conditions of raw material production, manufacture and distribution were restructured, as a result of an acceleration in the turnover of goods, a reduction in production costs and world-wide trade connections, which in turn produced changes in demand patterns. The traditional agrarian economic order, tied to family and custom, gradually changed into a consumer society modelled on the basis of industrial and rational criteria. Despite the continued division of Germany into different states, despite the strong monarchical police administration supported by landed property and the authority of princes and clerics, and despite the renovation of a quasi-absolutist constitutional state in the 1850s, the economy took on an increasingly dominant function in the political sphere. This became apparent both in the constitutional conflict in Prussia and in the national movement for political unity.

In this context it is vital to point to another consequence of the year 1848: the continuity of administrative efforts at reform, which in the years of the Vormärz[1] had been principally designed to achieve the aim of hoped-for industrial growth and which now in the years following the Vormärz emerged far more as a conservative force, as shown, for example, in the curtailment of legislation governing freedom of trade or in the support given to the attempts at amalgamation by threatened craft concerns. It was crucial that the protagonists of administrative reform nevertheless held fast to the principle of a liberal economic policy and pleaded, with the support of the manufacturers, merchants and agriculturalists, for the abolition of old constraints, for instance in the sphere of legislation on mining and in the field of commercial trade policy. Without doubt, the direct influence of the state receded, and yet without its liberal legislation the economic upswing could hardly have taken place. It provided the stimulus for, and facilitated, as one of a number of factors, the import of foreign capital into a country that relied extensively on cheap labour. This in turn was used to found new joint-stock companies (particularly in the western provinces) and to finance their industrial production. It also compelled the creation of a national trading state in Germany openly orientated towards the interests of Prussia. The first rough outlines of this state became visible during these years, in the conflict over the project for a Central

1. Vormärz – cf. footnote 6, Chapter 2.

European Customs Union, despite the opposition of Austria-Hungary and the South German states. Unimpressed by the protective needs of the Austrian economy, large-scale agricultural producers, wholesale merchants and the upper middle-class found a common denominator in the Customs Union in the concept of free trade, despite the opposition of industry and its wish for protective customs duties. It was recognised that the most important prerequisite for a general prosperity in the economy lay in the liberalisation of customs tariffs. The extent to which this realisation determined economic development can be ascertained by an examination of the boom of these years in the coal, iron and steel industries.

119 joint-stock companies were founded in Prussia between 1851 and 1857. Already by 1852 the Berlin Stock Exchange reported a 'very considerable and lively turnover in stocks and shares on internal and foreign accounts and for investment and speculation purposes'. If the Continent had clearly not suffered from a shortage of financial funds in 1850, this situation changed very quickly in the following years. In the wake of the liberalisation of iron-ore and coal mining, a multiplicity of concerns emerged in the Ruhr region involving, in part, considerable capital expenditure, at least for German conditions. They were followed by the foundation of firms in Upper Silesia, Bavaria, Württemberg and in the Saar region. Already by 1853 the stockbrokers in Berlin were able to verify that 'neither were supplies of shares available', 'nor could any purchases take place', as 'activity and adventurous inclination were so great in the industrial field'. In addition, there was a 'lively turn-over in the grain business'. Moreover the overseas import and export trade, which had been considerably expanded, absorbed large sums of money, so that the existing credit institutions were a long way from being in a position to meet the extent of contemporary requirements.

For these reasons it had been necessary from the very beginning, particularly in Prussia, to seek new ways of attracting capital in order to organise the concentrated utilisation of available funds. Indeed, this had to be achieved without the backing of a process of capital accumulation in foreign trade and a gradual extension of industrial concentration such as had taken place in England. The resources of the propertied class in Germany had proved to be too restricted, and the primary sector had shown little inclination to take a part in industrialisation and the re-channelling of capital reserves. The attempts of entrepreneurs to continue to finance the industrial upswing with their own credit and capital was doomed to failure in view of the rapid rate of economic growth. Therefore, even in the 1850s, they went to the public, with the intention of mobilising and collecting small and medium-sized capital assets in order to employ them lucratively in the industrial process. The share became a fashionable object. With the promise of a large increase in share prices and high dividends and rents, although frequently at the expense of wages, the banks successfully stimulated the foundation of firms. Nevertheless, all these efforts to transform liquid capital into industrial investments were not sufficient. Despite continued political complications within the Customs Union, this was a period of particularly active business dealing, substantial turnover in trade, 'very favourable conditions' and a 'great demand for money'. And so Germany remained dependent on foreign entrepreneurs and engineers, on foreign products and machines and on foreign capital, despite all its autononous achievements. Although the activity of the indigenous entrepreneur, German capital and cheap German labour constituted the basis for the upswing, without the stimulating effect of foreign assistance the prosperity of this short period, particularly in the under-capitalised western provinces, would not have been realised. Without the extraordinarily close connection of both private and joint-stock banks with France, Belgium and England, as well as the individual contacts of merchants and entrepreneurs with these countries, the immediate and high-risk application of innovations and the rationalised organisation of the large-scale concern which superseded in a few years the traditional form of the firm would not have been able to take place.

The Great Spurt: Imported Progress

The basic industries in Germany could compete only in a few specific sectors with the products of the already mature English economy; yet the three-fold increase in production in seven years, the roughly 40% rise in the size of the work force and the concentration on mass production showed that a demand existed which could be more or less satisfied by indigenous products. It was precisely the basic industries in Germany, which were only partially protected, that were forced to adopt a different approach to the one followed by their English counterparts. They were forced to seek their own sales markets, because they could participate in the extension of the European railway network only if they could undercut the English competition. Indeed this could be achieved only through a system of production that limited itself from the start to certain selected articles, which could, in addition, be sold cheaply because of the existence of relatively large organised concerns (for example Krupp's cast steel axle). Even during this first boom in the founding of firms, when the old sources of energy were gradually abandoned and new raw materials were required and exploited to a greater degree, organisational forms of manufacture became prominent which were essentially different from those in England. In addition, the comparative late start to industrial development had the advantage that the newest state of technology could be and indeed had to be adopted. Just as in the case of the banking mechanism, where changes in this direction had been enforced by the increasingly extensive demand for capital and the traditional distribution of land and property, the trend towards amalgamated concerns quickly became apparent at an early date in the case of the German coal, iron and steel industries. Large-scale manufacturing concerns appeared in the coal, iron and metallurgical sectors, which concentrated under one roof both production and distribution.

This development had its origins not only in the nature of individual markets and the financial conditions of the Customs Union: the traditions of the German industrial code also played an important role.

Although the family concern was superseded as a form

of production in the general economic upswing, it did not completely lose its significance. Many entrepreneurs were successful in achieving the leap towards greater output in the first phase of industrialisation. Although the necessary capital stock frequently had to be obtained and then secured by going public, the principle of the owner-director remained binding for the supervisory boards of the new concerns. The enlarged firms and even the joint-stock companies regarded themselves as constituting a clearly delineated area of authority, in which the community of production was at the same time a 'living community'. In principle they were completely organised according to the ideas of the feudal landowners in the provinces east of the Elbe, in the sense that the 'master of the factory', whether represented by the supervisory manager or the director, was responsible for the welfare of 'his' workers, and, at the same time, demanded their total devotion to 'his enterprise'. There therefore arose during these years a 'new form of feudalism', which was to be of great importance in the later conflicts concerning the leadership of the state.

As a result, on the one hand the pre-capitalist institutions, particularly in the sectors of iron and coal production, disappeared within a short space of time. On the other hand, the craft concerns – which had been transformed into fully-fledged factories – became the germinating seed for a new ruling consciousness of the industrial entrepreneurs.

The development in the textile industry was not very dissimilar to that in the machine industry. Equally in this case, mass demand and the supply of cheap and considerable quantities of American cotton forced a change to mass production and the abandonment of traditional methods. But in this sector, in contrast to the situation in the machine industry, the change meant at the same time a fierce conflict with the traditional putting-out system of domestic production, which was far less capable of carrying through the process of industrialisation. It was left to public companies and a few individual entrepreneurs to use rational methods of production and to direct the marketing policies of individual firms towards existing gaps in the Continental market.

But while industrial production was established in the coal, iron and textile industries, the application of new methods of production was only hesitantly implemented in the case of the chemical industry. Following a delay of half a century compared with English competitors, a start was made with basic research. Liebig, Kirchhoff, Bunsen, Winkler, Hofmann, Solvay and Kekule[2] developed the theory of benzene and chemical compounds, and their students and assistants experimented, if only within a narrow framework, with the production of dyes. The chemical industry developed a broader base, and the demand for its products rose with the general level of industrial production.

If one surveys the seven years of extensive industrial growth, which is commonly called the 'great spurt', it is apparent that the contribution of the Customs Union to the growth in world trade rose from 12.1 to 24.1 billion Taler. It is also apparent that the extent of increased production was in no way sufficient to meet demand. Germany was dependent for up to 50% of its needs on imports. The extensive new basic industries functioned largely with the help of foreign capital. In view of these conditions, there could be no discussion of an intensified protection of trade, which was demanded particularly by the industrialists. German production remained at the mercy of the superior English industries.

Although the epoch after the revolution was marked by unexpectedly substantial growth in industrial production, the beginnings of the shift in economic emphasis from the eastern to the western provinces and the continued division between the state and society, the politics and administration of the state remained rigidly dependent on the interests of the feudal aristocracy and landed property holders. No truly liberal policy emerged from the concentration of all the resources of the middle class on the promotion of industrial progress, science and technology.

2. See Appendix for biographies.

In fact, the traditional rights of the ruling elite of agricultural landlords were preserved; despite all the successes of the entrepreneurial class. Industrial change was, and remained, bound to the interests of large-scale agriculture. The 'great spurt' accelerated the pace of industrial growth. But notwithstanding this, the capitalist order did not achieve any ultimate success and, just as before, people felt themselves bound by duty to the ideology of the unity between the state and society. A consequence of this was that, after the experiences of 1848, political power 'remained in the final analysis out of the reach of the German middle class, unadjusted to its actual structure and therefore incorporating elements completely alien to its philosophy' (F. Zunkel). Despite an over-riding confidence and optimism, and amidst widespread belief in technical progress and manufacturing industry 'which is more important than every almshouse', the middle class accepted the 'concrete power of the state as the strongest authority in the political world' (H. Herzfeld). They were satisfied with their rising profits. Certainly the entrepreneurs did create new areas of authority to counterbalance their political impotence, in which middle-class thrift served as both a model and an example. At the same time, however, they desperately sought acceptance by the nobility and the monarchy. This necessarily involved a deliberate choice in favour of the further extension of feudalism in society. The mass of the population remained excluded from ownership of the means of production. The division between the feudal nobility and the increasingly feudalised middle class remained in existence even after 1848 and yet it was, above all, the gap which separated this group from the proletariat that was to determine the long-term course of German social history. This, then, is a further consequence of the events of 1848.

The events of 1848 had brought into being the social question and had led to the realisation of what 'speculative' commentators of the time had predicted. J. Droz formulated the situation as follows: 'To summarize, the German bourgeoisie was not in a position to understand the social problem which now emerged. Its awakening was to be all the more painful'. And the pain remained. From now on the 'social danger' was the theme of bourgeois demands for political freedom. This meant that the state, with its Christian and agricultural basis, could reduce to silence every demand for political freedom by pointing to the threat of revolution. Older traditions, and specifically those of enlightened absolutism, once again came to the forefront. These traditions had enabled Germany to become the defender of authoritarian ideologies prior to 1848, and they were to determine the country's development even after 'the monarchical and aristocratic powers were no longer able to fulfil the claims which they embodied' (K. Kehr). And so that which had been begun or had continued during the great spurt up until 1857 retained an element of ambivalence. Economic growth was matched by the restoration of traditional policies, and the *élan* of the entrepreneurial class by the predominance of a corporative ideology. The economic rise of the German middle class, both in industry and trade became radically divorced, as it were, from its socio-political development (W. Zorn). While the nobility and monarchy continued to be the leaders of the life of the state, the broad class of workers and peasants were simply seen as a reservoir of cheap labour. This development became most visibly acute as the first great boom in the Customs Union in 1857 suddenly turned into a short, sharp crisis. Although the crisis originated in America, the consequences for the German economy were to be of a similar significance to those of the crises of 1873 and 1929.

4

The Breakthrough:
the Foundation of the
German Economy

In March 1825 Friedrich Harkort emphasised in eloquent words his hope for 'a quick and cheap conveyancing of goods' with the help of the railways, and had wished 'that the time would also soon come in the Fatherland, when the triumphal train of industrial diligence would be harnessed to smoking giants and blaze a trail for the public spirit'. Half a century later these wishes had already been fulfilled in a startling fashion. Even if by the end of the 1860s development had not quite reached the 'English level', Friedrich Engel's analysis, which had been derived from mid-century conditions in England, nevertheless accurately reflected the industrial revolution that was taking place in Germany. 'The bourgeoisie' had also created in Germany 'more massive and colossal forces of production than all previous generations put together. The subjugation of natural power, the use of machinery, the application of chemistry to industry and agriculture, steam-shipping, railways, the electric telegraph, the new cultivation of complete parts of the world, the process of making rivers navigable and the creation of whole populations – what earlier centuries had imagined that such forces of production lay dormant in the lap of society?' Germany had also taken part in the 'period of promotion and speculation' in the years after 1850, 'which

The Foundation of the German Economy

were dominated by the development of productive forces until then unimagined'. They were characterised 'by the progressive realignment of all aspects of life on an economic footing and by the creation of new types of economic organisations of a specifically capitalist nature' (H. Rosenberg).

But in contrast to its western neighbours, in Germany the bourgeoisie did not come to power. The 'feudal, patriarchal, and idyllic conditions' (F. Engels) were not destroyed. In fact, just the opposite was the case. Probably the German land-owning class had an 'instinctive foreboding that the locomotive was the hearse on which absolutism and feudalism would be carried to the churchyard' (F. Harkort), but in contrast to the situation in England and France, the German aristocracy were able to channel the dynamism of the entrepreneurial middle-class forces and themselves to take the step towards large-scale agricultural production on a capitalist basis. The reason for this can be found not only in the specific historical tradition of the German territories, but also in the interval between the trends in industrial and agricultural growth – an interval particular to German development. Until the last third of the nineteenth century, this lag between the trend cycles of industry and agriculture affected economic and social development in a completely decisive way, and enabled the aristocracy time and again to gain a breathing-space in order to secure the old order. In contrast, the industrial boom was continuously drawn into the whirlpool of crisis and depression, which was partly of a local nature and of short duration, but also in part world-wide and long-lasting.

This situation was highlighted quite clearly during and after the crisis of 1857, which followed the phase of over-speculation and over-production during the Crimean War. It hit Germany at the peak of the speculative fever in shares during the initial boom in the economy. Without any doubt, the roughly 30% fall in the wholesale price index in the Customs Union severely shook the wholesale trade and the large-scale agricultural producers. But the effect on newly-emergent industries of the shrinkage in volume

46

and turnover in both freight, rail and sea traffic was even more adverse. It proved to be of decisive importance that, while the trading sector and the agriculturalists were able to raise their turnover again relatively quickly because of rising prices, the boom was followed by a period of stagnation in industry. Because foreign capital had been withdrawn from Germany during the crisis, the attempts at rationalisation had largely been made at the cost of the broad section of speculators. Confidence in industrial progress vanished. Although the procedure of 'combining a private allocation of profits with a social responsibility for losses' (H. Rosenberg) had proved itself effective as a cure for the crisis, the shock over the fragility of the 'joint-stock company as the organisation form of the economic order' continued in the first instance to influence the stock exchange. The business of speculation with industrial stocks had fallen into discredit for leading state officials as well as for the majority of the middle class. The banks also became more cautious. This resulted in a situation where the factories had to meet the crisis with their own resources. With the help of a reduction in dividends and capital and by means of rationalisation and amalgamation, they had not only to defend their technical achievements, but also to introduce technological innovations, and in particular the new Bessemer process, without the availability of external sources of credit.

The crisis, therefore, brought about forcibly the first clarification of market conditions. It in no way destroyed the concerns which had emerged during the upswing, but it reduced to a considerable extent the speculative offshoots, and considerably damaged the competitive ability of hand-operated industries and craft concerns. Thus, the crisis indirectly created the prerequisite for the erection of new industrial concerns.

The crisis had a similar effect on the banks. They began to devote themselves to the regular business of banking, and returned once more to the traditional business of dealing in government securities. They gave their support to the wholesale trade and developed a geographically decentralised, but structurally concentrated, system of deposit banking. Whereas the private banks continued as before to concentrate primarily on business financing, the joint-stock banks in Cologne and Berlin began to extend their deposit transactions. This restructuring of business activity resulted in an increase in foreign investment which enabled the banks, in conjunction with a new industrial upswing in the 1860s, to undertake many diversified activities.

The renewed economic upswing which reached its peak in 1873 was closely connected with the emergence of an enclosed and nationally unified German economic area. This development was itself indirectly connected with the crisis of 1857. During the upswing of the 1850s, both the political and economic situation in Germany had been dominated by the tenacious and embittered struggle between Austria and Prussia for the continued leadership of the Customs Union. In the course of the conflict over the projected central European Customs Union, the German national state took shape. This occurred as a result of the effective foundation of an economic order over this area, based on free-trade and therefore western european principles. Even up to the crisis of 1857, the conflict had remained by no means resolved. Austria could always still hope to extend the trade agreement of 1853 with Prussia into a Customs Union, with the aim of breaking Prussia's influence in the fullest way possible. After the crisis, however, it became increasingly apparent that Prussia, rather than Austria, was in a position to overcome the period of economic stagnation by means of a liberal economic policy. The Austrian Empire suffered from the repercussions of its adventurous involvement in the Crimean War, and the defeats in Italy compelled it to give up the attempted reconciliation with Prussia through increasing liberalisation and to turn towards protection. The small mid-German states did not want to participate in this change, as their interests lay increasingly in the North between the Elbe and the Rhine.

The economic upswing of the 1850s only produced positive political advantages for Prussia. Austria attempted, unsuccessfully, from 1859 to 1864 to harness this development in the interest of obtaining a protective customs area covering Austria and greater Germany. Prussia, conscious of its own aims, began to seek economic connections with France, Belgium and England, in order to force through a 'little German' solution to the existing problems. Supported by the agrarian and trading sectors and their mutual interest in a further liberalisation of tariffs, the Prussian government, even before Bismarck's appointment, understood how to capitalise on the economic interconnections of the small and medium-sized states with Prussia in the Customs Union. Prussia also knew how to use to the full extent its economic and industrial superiority within the German Confederation, particularly as it did not have to take into consideration the needs of its own industrial sector for tariff protection. Prussia, which with the Ruhr, Upper Silesia and the Saar region contributed over 90% of the output of the mining and metal industries of the Customs Union in 1865, was finally able to outstrip its Austrian antagonist and model German economic development according to its own interests. Help in the sphere of trading policy was provided up to 1864 by France and England. As a result, the remaining members of the Customs Union were compelled to adapt themselves to Prussia and to accept Prussia's liberal legislation in the economic sphere. In the early 1860s freedom of trade and employment was introduced into the individual states of the Customs Union and their economies were organised according to the Prussian model. For the mid-German states after 1864 there was, in the words of King Ludwig of Bavaria, 'no other choice'. Compelled 'by powerful interests' they were forced 'to seek a connection with Prussia'.

The initial framework for the future form of the Empire was thereby provided. After the exclusion of Austria from the Customs Union and the binding of the Customs Union to Prussia, the political unification of 'little Germany' seemed only a question of time. However the relatively slower development of the economy provided no excuse for the brutality of the tactics employed by Bismarck in his attempt to achieve the political fulfilment of this policy.

The Foundation of the German Economy

With the conclusion of the French trading treaty, Prussia, in the words of the later director of the German Bank, Georg von Siemens, 'had gone over to the western European system' and now constituted 'a country, as did France and England'.

> And we want to preserve our position vis-à-vis these competitors, who are ahead of us in capital and power, and not let ourselves be relegated to the status of a colony, such as Portugal, Turkey and Jamaica etc. If we don't want to become a purely agricultural nation, with our products replaced by English goods, and we ourselves subject to direct plunder, then we must have Schleswig-Holstein, and the Customs Union must be identical with Prussia.

Both of these demands were achieved with the luck of the successful diplomacy of Bismarck who was conscious in all his moves of the economic power and extraordinary industrial growth of Prussia.

This growth and this power were, for their part, impelled forward and supported by the successful policy of Bismarck. The prospect of a larger and unified German economic area had once more revived entrepreneurial energies. Despite the intensified political conflicts between Prussia's conservative system and the claims of the liberal middle class, the stock exchange in Berlin reported at the beginning of the 1860s 'a profitable utilisation of money', 'extremely favourable successes', a 'continuing upswing' and 'confidence' in Bismarck. A lively trade in bills of exchange and securities developed on a substantial scale, fuelled by increasing investments and a rising turnover in goods. Berlin capital was once again involved in industrial firms, although certainly no longer from a purely speculative point of view, and it helped to concentrate the accumulated capital of joint-stock companies in the western provinces and in the emerging growth industries of chemical and electrical engineering production. The final integration of the Customs Union with the 'western trading system' also meant the start of extensive business concentration in Prussia along capitalist lines, the process being initiated from Berlin. This also created the prerequisite for a rapid recovery from stagnation. Existing capital held in foreign hands was to a large extent nationalised. The energetic promotion of railway construction, the further extension of trading routes, and the dramatic rise in the volume of goods transported also led to a considerable increase in coal-mining and iron-ore and iron production. As a result, the process of reconstruction after the 1857–60 crisis enabled the simultaneous financing of technical innovations and the application of more intensive methods of production. The gulf between German and English production was closed. Within the Customs Union, Prussian production began to overtake the output levels of French and Belgian industries. When, in the middle of this decade, the problem of a shortage of capital reappeared, it became apparent that the simplification of the monetary system effected in the 1850s was instrumental in preventing any threat to the economy as a whole. Of equal importance in this context had been the unification of customs tariffs, the removal of customs payments on river transport and the reorganisation of the banking mechanism. In addition, the succesful wars of Prussia had emphatically altered the investment habits of the public. A grest deal of capital was transferred from the traditional areas of investment in state securities, and particularly in Austrian loans, to the high interest-bearing sectors of Prussian industry; and this accelerated the development of the future market structure which was to be typical for Germany, with its centre in Berlin. A first step had been taken towards the concentration of capital, and a further step towards the structural division of the country between the industrialised, thoroughly capitalised and urbanised West and the agriculturally oriented, capital-deficient East. For the time being, this development did not lead to any conflict worth mentioning, as the agricultural boom, the speculative investments following the abolition of estate taxes and the continuing industrialisation of the primary sector made possible the auto-financing of aristocratic and landed property. In any case, political developments within Germany offered adequate compensation for those searching for power.

The Prussian victory of 1866 was a victory of the Taler over the Gulden, and it initiated a period of increased economic activity. The Prussian entrepreneurs sought to bind the indebted South to the Prussian state. Even in the 1850s, capital from South Germany had financed innovations in Prussia, but from now on this was completely out of the question. Rothschild and most of the private banks in South Germany as well as in Prussia lost their commanding position. To an increasing extent, the joint-stock banks came to dominate the business of state loans. They were preparing themselves to take over the leadership in the sphere of credit and financial policy in the emergent state.

And yet industrial growth after 1866 was not exclusively the result of private entrepreneurial initiative. It was also the result of the economic policies implemented in Prussia and North Germany. Because the rapid and direct assimilation of the South had failed, Prussia abandoned the economic and political possibilities of a 'policy of unity', and intensified the economic development of the North German organisation of states under the leadership of the 'Chief of the General Staff of the free-traders', Rudolph von Delbrück. This policy was implemented according to the principles of free-trade, with a view to public opinion in Germany and the Southern states. It is true that this policy, which was to prepare the way for national unity, with the help of a German Customs Parliament, failed – due to the opposition of the South German states to 'enforced quiescence, payment of taxes and military conscription'. But the rather superficial political moves of the governments of these states could not prevent the final rupture of the craft system by the principle of free competition.

By means of 84 laws, 40 treaties and numerous presidial decrees, Delbrück succeeded, in collaboration with the liberal forces in Prussia, in making the North German Imperial Diet the bearer of economic liberalism. The standardisation of weights and measures followed on from the standardisation of trade laws and the creation of a supreme law court for trading matters, with its seat in Leipzig. Further developments involved new legislation on industry, and finally, the ratification of the North German criminal law code. In particular, dealings in shares were made much easier, and the repeal of the duty of registration on the setting-up of joint-stock companies was decreed. As a result, the 'caring' interference of the state in the process of industrialisation and the development of capitalism, which had often had a retarding effect, was finally renounced.

It was only now that the middle class, in alliance with the administration, succeeded in breaking the historical narrowness of Prussia and North Germany, thereby providing the legal basis on which the massive boom of 1871–73 was able to develop. For only with the repeal of the duty of registration was lucrative business activity by the large banking concerns made possible, and the liberal, free-trade framework was provided within which new foundations in the banking and industrial sectors could develop.

But it was not only business companies and banks who found this legislation of the utmost significance. It also marked the beginning of a period of intensive capital connections between high finance and heavy industry, and initiated the involvement of banks in the industrial sector and intensified the trend already laid down in the conditions of competition and marketing in Germany towards the integrated concern and industrial concentration. The new law marked the end of the ideological concept of the 'whole house'.

From now on, the process of modernisation within the state became increasingly fragmented and diverse, and the growing degree of tension was to determine further development.

The changes in the relationship between the state and the individual, which had been introduced by Stein and Hardenberg, had found their natural conclusion. After the abolition of hereditary serfdom at the beginning of the nineteenth century and the dismantling of the 'principle of direction' in the mid century, the authoritarian state finally renounced the last instruments of state management, by means of the law permitting free movement of labour and the assurance of freedom of trade. The State now limited itself to the creation of equal conditions of employment and competition and left the initiative and leadership of the productive capitalist economy in the hands of manufacturers, bankers and wholesale merchants.

This legislation, however, was significant in a different sense: it was the final phase of a policy against which the Prussian landed aristocracy had campaigned since the beginning of the century. In the final analysis, however, the aristocracy had to accept this policy as the only means by which the traditional division of power in the state could be retained. That is to say, the German middle class, which had been deflected into the sphere of industrial activity after 1848, had been revitalised, and had begun to press again for its traditional goals of political freedom and German unity, either with or without the support of Prussia. Prussia had initially attempted successfully to combine the aims of the National Association (founded in 1859) with its own policies, but the more prominent the conflict between parliamentary and authoritarian leadership became in Prussia, the more fragile this accord became. It became increasingly unlikely that the coalition of a feudal aristocracy and the middle class, which had been founded in 1848, could retain a common function. In this situation the economic prosperity of the 1860s assumed outstanding significance. It enabled the Prussian government to achieve two important things. In the First place, it made it possible to continue to combine both liberal and conservative claims on the basis of mutually-adjusted material interests, without needing to alter the existing power relationship. Secondly, it enabled the Prussian government to cultivate the divisions within the middle-class camp, following the implementation of free trade and the foundation of pro-Prussian associations which bound the active resources of the entrepreneurial

The Foundation of the German Economy

class to Prussia as the prime economic power in Germany. Despite all political opposition, it had stimulated economic co-operation. 'Let politics die', so it was said, 'and political economics alone will seize the newly gained ground'!

This development received enormous impetus from the wars. The year 1864 brought a form of agreement with Bismarck's middle-class opponents, and after 1866, sustained by military victories, he could make his peace with the representatives of the people. Certainly this policy created a division not only among the liberals, but also in the conservative camp. At the same time, however, new parties of specific interest groups were formed, the majority of whom – for economic considerations – were not prepared to oppose Prussia's rise to power by means of the unification of Germany. Bismarck was the idol of the supporters of a prestigious national and economic policy, and this made it possible for the celebrated man of the 'German movement' once more to combine liberal ideas and conservative interests on all issues where the demands of the protagonists overlapped. These included free trade and the shaping of an economic order along liberal, industrial and capitalist lines.

On this basis and in the shadow of state power in Prussia the new constitution of the North German Union emerged. On the one hand it was linked with the traditions of the 'Paulskirche'.[1] On the other hand, however, it was clearly modelled in the interests of Prussia. Bismarck was concerned above all with the need to strengthen the power of the state, and this meant ensuring a decisive influence for the feudal aristocracy and the landed interest. Neither the people, nor majority opinion, nor constitutional rights counted for Bismarck, who only accepted the primacy, the authority and the law of the state. Prussia was still an agricultural nation, as were most of the other areas of Germany, and the noble supporters of the Prussian system still knew how to achieve their own ends. The liberals had

1. The 'Paulskirche' was the church of St Paul, which was the meeting-place of the Frankfurt Parliament. At its first meeting (18 May 1848), 330 delegates were in attendance.

to be comforted by the creation of a Parliament chosen according to democratic principles. This in fact amounted to very little, but it was something all the same, since now at least the possibility of 'influential counsel' appeared to have been established. The constitution which Bismarck had graciously presented was accepted. The liberals hoped for the unity of the nation and believed that, with unity, political freedom would also be achieved.

But this did not materialise, even with the founding of the Empire. It was a unity gained by force of arms, established by the princes and the free cities by a 'voluntary agreement' and proclaimed on foreign soil. This unity, which was nonetheless joyfully greeted by many sections of the population, did not signify any epoch-making caesura in the economic, social or political history of Germany. The inherited structures remained. The decisions of 1815, 1848, 1862 and 1866 were reinforced, and the 'decisive role of the leading groups in Prussia and the agricultural provinces east of the Elbe' (W. Zorn), and their dominant relationship with the middle class and other groups in society, was effectively sanctioned.

The dazzling splendour of the military successes made it possible for Bismarck to make secure to a large extent — both in foreign and domestic politics — the power structure of the throne, nobility, army and bureaucracy. Above all, the financial sovereignty of the territories was preserved, the imperial administration being merely concerned with economic matters. Further, the officials of the Empire were simply to fulfil their duties under the aegis of the imperial chancellor, who was not responsible to the elected Parliament. The 'fourth estate' remained completely excluded from the planned structure of the state, and no place could be found for it either in conservative or liberal thought. Both groups regarded its problems as being of a moral nature, involving questions of religion, and attempts were therefore made to alleviate the economic difficulties of the fourth estate through education and training 'in a way corresponding to the eternal rules of social intercourse'. For this reason the worker associations, with their revolutionary demands originating from the writings of Born, Weitling[2] and communism, had been summarily prohibited. This was designed to put a stop to the politicisation of the working class and to neutralise their ambitions by channelling their activities into the unpolitical denominational workers' associations, as they had been outlined by Ketteler, Kolping and Wichern.[3] The working-class movement had recognised the need for an organised class war, and although the opposition remained dispersed in a variety of different groups after the defeat of 1848, the organisation of a new class was completed with the breakthrough of the industrial system. In this context, an important factor was the creation of new employment opportunites through the process of industrial growth. Although the long periods of work and social insecurity threatened the very existence of the working class, just as before, the majority – who also saw their interests represented by liberalism – supported the little-Germany and pro-Prussian policies of the liberals. Economic demands receded to a large extent into the background. Even the other tradition of class warfare which had been established by Marx and then directed by Liebknecht and Bebel differed far less from the movement led by Lassalle in its social and revolutionary aims, than in its anti-Prussian attitude and its approach to the greater German problem. In the 1860s the working-class movement had had a distinctive political identity, which had been moulded not least by the fact that the imported economic advance was accompanied by an equally prominent export of social tensions. Almost two million Germans left their homeland.

The situation seemed relaxed. A working-class movement loyal to the state had, in the 1860s, pushed the revolutionary ideas of 1848 well into the background. The Communist Manifesto, although studied with suspicion, was used above all by the conservatives as a tactical political instrument. The workers were committed just as much as the middle class to the concept of nationalism and yet they were cut off from the middle-class standard of

2. See Appendix for biographies.
3. See Appendix for biographies.

living and were forced as before into obedience. They
strove for the creation of a bourgeois democracy by means
of reform 'through the work of enlightening the people
and the achievement of a majority in Parliament' (H. Gre-
bing). The campaign for emancipation was only revived
when it became clear that the working class had failed to
obtain a share either in the process of political decision-
making, or in the economic boom. Only then did a
uniform, self-conscious class movement, organised along
Trade Union lines, begin to emerge from the politically
divided workers' associations, which had been largely
tied to provincial areas and stratified according to professional status. It had been precisely these associations
that had constituted the, mass basis of support for the
liberal party. The new movement began to question to an
increasing extent the social and political order that was
established in 1871. In that year its voice was without
weight, but in a country where a successful revolution had
never taken place, this development was merely a reflection of historical consistency.

The proclamation of the Emperor and the Empire finally
persuaded the majority of the population, and in particular the liberal German nationalists, to side with Prussia
in political affairs. The particularism of the South German
states and the democratic parliamentary opposition were
both silenced remarkably quickly in the face of the general
enthusiasm for the re-creation of the Empire. The population of the new Empire accepted the Prussian tradition as
genuinely German. National enthusiasm for the unity
which had finally been achieved went hand in hand with
delight over the advantages of the 'policy of economic
fulfilment' implemented by Delbrück. The war and the
war boom stimulated the economy. Freed from political
risks and stimulated by the massive French war reparation
payments, prosperity led directly to a rapid upswing in
economic growth. In less than three years Germany had
achieved complete integration in the sphere of western
European industrial production.

Until 1873, an economic boom took place in Germany
which was marked by a reciprocal magnification of many

world-wide factors involving an effective acceleration in sales and production. In the process of this development, Berlin, which now possessed its own machine construction industry, became the fulcrum between the Ruhr and Upper Silesia. Along this axis – the Ruhr–Berlin–Upper Silesia – the great credit transactions of the joint-stock banks developed, which on the one hand freed the German economy from dependence on foreign stock markets and on the other hand pushed the private banks further into the background and thereby determined the future form of industrial development in Germany. New interest groups were formed, and industrial concerns emerged of a size never before equalled. At the same time the manager took over the position of the owner-director, and the limited company replaced the family concern. In most cases industrial expansion involved the raising of share capital and the foundation and restructuring of new firms. As a result, this second boom accelerated the structural changes in the German economy. Only the joint-stock banks were in a position to fund the high-risk promotion of mergers, such as the Gelsenkirchen Mining Company, or to provide the capital for the restructuring of numerous companies in the building, trade and railway sectors. In these years alone, 857 concerns were founded and only the banks were capable of solving the problem of the 'organic connection of turnover and business investment with the possibility of securing a continuous supply of indigenous funds'. Only that form of organisation which was itself an object of speculation remained equal to the growing need for capital.

The promoters of industrial concentration regarded the Empire and its military role as providing a completely secure sales market for the outstanding increase in production. Furthermore there was a common expectation implicit in these activities that the exploitation of the newly-created economic potential could be achieved in the context of rising prices and the absence of any threatening crisis.

But this hope quickly proved to be illusory. Already in 1873 the overheated boom was transformed into a severe and continuous depression, which placed in doubt the stability of the new concerns. On the other hand, the slump contributed to the strengthening of the new industrial order. During the boom period it had become increasingly apparent that heavy industry had taken over first place in the economic life of Prussia and Germany as a whole. At the same time industrial strikes seemed to intensify the danger of a social revolution. This dual development provides the reason why the crisis in the economic order of 1873 became one that involved the power structure of the new state. This crisis in its turn was the rock upon which economic and political liberalism was to founder.

The breakthrough of the capitalist system in Germany had taken place under the aegis of liberalism and the ideas of autonomous free trade. But, at the pinnacle of the success of these principles (marked by the transition to the gold standard and the foundation of the Imperial Bank), the movement collapsed following the opposition of those equally revived forces which demanded a reactivation of the protectionist policies of state mercantilism. Even during the period of the Empire's foundation, at a time of great economic growth and upheaval, the authoritative traditions of feudalism and agriculture had never been broken. The ambivalence of German development had merely been disguised by the national question. Tensions and conflict broke out again with great violence once the economic boom had been transformed into a crisis. As a consequence, the position of those forces that had supported the state was seriously shaken. But the solution applied by Bismarck and the government to this problem created in its turn a new dilemma in Germany, which was not to be overcome until the middle of the following century.

5

The Great Crisis:
the Re-Establishment of the Economic and Social Order

In 1849 the Rhineland and Westphalia had 651 stationary steam engines with an output of 18,775 horsepower. By 1875, there were 11,706 engines with 379,091 horsepower. In 1847 the length of the Prussian railway network had stood at 2,754 km.; in 1875 Prussia controlled a functioning and integrated railway network with a total length of 16, 169 km. By about 1850 Essen had 9,000 inhabitants; this had risen by 1875 to almost 55,000, equivalent to an increase of 628% in total population. This not only provides a picture of the rapid growth of Prussian industry in the Ruhr region, but also highlights the concentration of the new industries in the Western provinces. It also reflects the productive capacity of the new economic order emerging after the 1850s. While the bank-note circulation in Prussia around 1850 was reported as being still only 18 million Taler, by 1875 the circulation was 290 million Taler. The number of foundations of new concerns based on share capital also provides an indication why turnover had increased so rapidly and where German capital had flowed. 857 companies, with a share capital of over 1.4 million Taler, were created in the years 1871–4 alone. Over 500,000 workers found employment in more than 11,000 concerns, each employing more than 5 workers. The labour-force in the mines rose from 12,741 to 83,000 workers, and coal production increased eight-fold, pig iron production fourteen-fold and steel production 54-fold.

The upswing in production and the breakthrough of modern industrialism could not be doubted. Germany had matched England, the first industrial nation in the world, in the decisive sectors of industrial growth, in railway construction, coal consumption, and the application of steam power and engines, in iron production and in the demand for raw cotton. It had abandoned its traditions, built up its own efficient banking mechanism and had often participated in a leading role in the sphere of technical advance. Germany had in fact pressed forward with the extension and concentration of industry to such an extent that it had surpassed the English prototype, without destroying the basic agricultural structure of its national economy. Indeed, in contrast to the situation in England, industrial and agricultural growth had taken place simultaneously. Also in contrast to England, the possibilities for technical change had been by no means exhausted by the 1870s; the railway system was still imcomplete and the reservoir of labour as yet untapped. Indeed these resources and prerequisites for industrial development remained preserved, despite the long-term stagnation which set in with the great depression of 1873, which not only introduced the second phase of technical change in Germany, but also brought to a conclusion the extension of concerns founded in the first phase.

As in the case of the boom, the depression was divided into two stages sharply differentiated from each other. Both, however, were to be significant in the further development of the German economy, as during this fresh period of delayed growth (as had been the case prior to 1848) the technical and organisational prerequisites were created which were to serve as the basis for new growth. For example, during the first phase, which lasted in Germany until 1879, the international price level for goods fell dramatically – without, however, restricting the movement towards expansion and concentration, or producing a fall in production levels. At the same time, interest groups emerged which stimulated a radical change in the economic and political sphere from the individualism of middle-class liberalism to protectionism and the 'group solidarity of the age of mass production' (K. E. Born). They thereby fostered the structural reorganisation of the Prussian and German states. The long period of economic stagnation and moderate growth which followed this phase and lasted until the mid 1890s brought the changes already under way to their final conclusion and led to the compulsory restructuring of industry. Whereas all energies prior to 1879 had been devoted to general economic policy, the 1880s marked a radical reassessment of traditional business methods, ways of thinking and forms of organisation. Although the degree of change varied in individual sectors of the economy, the principle of individual leadership of a concern and autonomous political action was increasingly abandoned in favour of corporative action. With the help of agreements, and partly by means of short-term amalgamation, it was hoped that similar aims could be more effectively and readily achieved. Without any doubt the prerequisite for these decisions on amalgamation was the transition to protective tariffs which took place in 1879, and yet despite this the two phases of the great depression cannot be judged as one phenomenon. On the contrary, they must be interpreted as two specific economic and social processes, which were to influence the political situation in different ways. The 1870s were marked by the discrediting of liberalism; the 1880s by the discrediting of conservatism.

If one examines the direct economic consequences of the crisis, it can be established that, as in the case of the 1857 crisis, although it induced strains in the industrial system, it did not destroy it. Rather, the crisis cemented the new order. As early as 1874 the Berlin banks could speak of the depression in terms of its being 'a transition period which was useful for curing existing moral and material damage' (G. v. Siemens). Even after the catastrophe at the end of 1873, the joint-stock company remained the model for the structure of concerns in the German economy. In the intervening period – and this was to be of great consequence for later economic development – the crisis had destroyed the economic viability of numerous small-scale firms and unsound new foundations, thereby creating the basis on which the large associations of capital and productive capacity would be able to build.

This tendency was immediately apparent, particularly in the banking sector. Only a few banks succeeded in quickly overcoming the crisis, despite heavy losses on the balance sheets and a heavy involvement in the founding of firms. The majority of these banks were centred in Berlin, and they either had a secure clientele, as in the case of the Disconto-Gesellschaft, the Darmstädter Bank and the Berlin Handelsgesellschaft, or had not been intensely involved in domestic speculation, but had found a secure business in trade and export, as in the case of the Deutsche Bank and the Dresdner Bank. On the other hand, many of the provincial banks, which were often better secured financially, went bankrupt. The Berlin banks accordingly benefited from a high quotation on the stock market and this in turn led to an extension in their influence. They took over the remaining liquid assets from the mass of bankruptcies of 1873 and extended their connections throughout the whole of Germany. By the mid 1870s a handful of joint-stock banks centred in Berlin held almost undisputed sway over the German capital market. The process of centralisation and concentration had begun. From now on the provincial and private banks, including even the larger ones such as Bleichröder, Rothschild, Warschauer, Oppenheim etc., came increasingly under the influence of the Berlin banks. During the 1870s, the latter covered Germany with a network of branches, with the aim of concentrating German capital resources in Berlin. By these means they hoped to be able to lend their support to what was regarded as a 'reasonable and timely' development towards large-scale concerns.

None of the concerns receiving support from the Berlin banks was forced to go into liquidation. Although the banks once more gave priority after 1873 to regular business and gave increased attention to fiscal considerations, they remained extensively involved in industry. Indeed, the crisis bound the banks even more closely to the expanded and integrated concerns threatened by the depression. In addition the great trading banks, such as the Deutsche Bank and the Dresdner Bank, which until now had operated without any permanent industrial clientele, moved into new markets and established themselves in the coal, iron and steel sectors. The results of such concentration were many. Through the integration of many concerns (often only recently founded) into a few large joint-stock companies, 'good money was earned'. Further, in the words of Rosencrantz, director of the Dresdner Bank, a 'diligent, highly educated and capable management, endowed with energy and will' was able to rise to positions of leadership in the German economy. Indeed, within the German economy the building trade had experienced a 27-fold increase in share capital; the bank sector a nine-fold increase in size and the metal-working industry a seven-fold rise in production. Thus the crisis of 1873, through the process of selection and concentration, had effectively reduced the small circle of those responsible for exercising influence of German economic development and German politics.

The intimate connections between the banks and industry which had been intensified by the crisis had an important side-effect for Germany. In view of the severe crisis in production and the drastic fall in prices, the banks saw themselves compelled to declare their solidarity with the demand for a protective tariff for Germany's basic industries. It was argued that these could no longer maintain their position against the competition of English industries which had been equally threatened by the crisis and had responded with a policy of dumping and underpriced exports. And so it came about that the German Banks, although maintaining an interest in free market conditions and indeed remaining international in their business connections, became as far as their banking and political aims were concerned purely 'national concerns'. The banks also hoped that an increased volume of production, obtained by means of a reserved internal market, would both improve their balance sheets and enable them to extend their overseas business in order to facilitate the replacement of London as the agent for German trade and merchandise. Economic nationalism served to bring the banks and the basic industries together; and both found additional support from the south German textile industry, which found itself threatened by a crisis of over-production compounded by the annexation of Alsace and Lorraine. Together they formed a united front in strict opposition to free trade and liberal policies.

Already by the end of 1874 the iron, steel and textile industries had decided to create organisational support for their agitation, in the form of a new union of interested parties which would cover the whole of Germany, such as the Association of German Iron and Steel Industrialists. Indeed, this type of agitation could not be performed by the previous pressure groups, which tended to be localised and tied to a specific industrial sector. In 1874 the industrialists began to break the unity of interest among free-traders in the Chambers of Commerce, in the Congress of Economists and in the German Handelstag. As unlimited freedom of trade failed to secure any success, the 'largely thoughtless worship of, and belief in, the natural harmonisation of the market mechanism gradually lost its hypnotic power' (H. Rosenberg). But despite this, the protagonists of the new economic nationalism did not succeed in taking the place of the 'fading community of interest of free-traders as a new inner force behind German integration' (W. Zorn). The free-traders still acted as agents between the Prussian East and the Prussian and German oriented South and West, supported by a coalition of administrators, wholesale traders, agriculturalists and the middle class. The basic consensus of national interest and the policies of Bismarck were shaped according to this situation.

Three events finally helped the opposition of heavy industry to success in the 1870s and made possible the reform of the newly-founded state. In the first place, nascent industries benefited increasingly from the extraordinary growth in population in rural areas evident from the end of the 1860s onwards. This in turn acted as a stimulant for economic development. Emigration gave way to internal migration and a regrouping within society between the countryside and the city and between East and West. The western provinces of Prussia, previously characterised by a lower birth rate than the Eastern provinces, now took over the leading role in determining the overall rate of population growth. This emergent transference of population from the East to the West took place at the same time as a general reduction in wages and mass dismissals of workers in the Western provinces. The 'social question' became once again a vital contemporary issue. From the class struggle of small activist elements under the leadership of political parties, there had emerged a uniform and organised working class with radical political and revolutionary social aims. Although it would be probably incorrect to speak in terms of a mass movement, the demands of the radicals became increasingly influential. The fact that the united activities of the General Association of German Workers and the Social Democratic Workers Party had gained many more supporters in the period after 1875 than had the parallel efforts of the Christian parties could no longer be kept secret. With their Gotha programme, the former group aimed at 'breaking the iron law of wages by abolishing the system of wage labour'. They equally aimed at 'the removal of all forms of exploitation and the ending of all social and political inequality'. The Social Democrats wanted to establish their 'People's State' only by legal means, and they certainly were not anarchists or even terrorists, but their programme nonetheless threatened the structure and form of Bismarck's state in its entirety.

Secondly, agricultural growth reached its peak in the mid 1870s and then came to a standstill. The intensive system of crop rotation and machine cultivation of land had certainly led to a considerable increase in yields per hectare, but intensive arable cultivation also meant rising costs per unit of production. German agriculture, with its high production costs, was in danger of losing the competitive race with 'low cost, extensive cultivation in East-

67

ern Europe and was in a worse position in comparison with the production costs of agriculture on the virgin soils on the other side of the ocean' (G. Stolper). By the mid 1870s a critical situation had been reached: the export boom was reversed. Prussia could no longer compete with overseas producers, because of the extension of the railway network in the USA and the increased competition between steamship lines, which had produced a roughly 75% fall in transport costs. As a result German agriculture became dependent on the home market, which in turn was threatened by cheap foreign grain. The conditions of competition in the primary sector had changed completely. At the same time the new system of provincial and local administration organised along liberal lines radically disturbed the patriarchal position of estate-holders, who saw both their economic position and their political influence in danger. On the basis of such considerations the agriculturalists for their part joined together in 1876 in pressure groups, in order to protect themselves from the automatic operation of world market prices by means of collective political efforts. With the help of protective tariffs they believed that they would be able to prevent the further extension of the capitalist system. On the basis of 'Christian fairness and justice', they wanted to push through a 'moral reinvigoration of old traditional social norms and static ideals of life' and enforce 'the partial reintroduction of extinct estate-orientated, corporative and controlled economic systems, which would be protected against the stock exchange, the world market and other disturbers of the peace'. They hoped to bring into effect 'a reorganisation and stabilisation of the economic, social and political importance of the various classes, which was modelled on the past at the direct cost of "mobile capital" which had become so hated and its hangers-on' (H. Rosenberg). In their eyes, the 'constitutional state founded on law and justice' had had its day. According to von Knebel-Döberitz 'we must return to the so-called patrimonial and patriarchal state'. Although their programme was visibly directed against industry and the banks, they did share common ground with these groups in their fear of their 'mutual social antagonist' and their combined 'interest in a joint social and internal policy based on conservative principles'; and both wished for an end to the 'freedom of the economy from state involvement, and the adoption of a policy of state economic protection' (K. E. Born).

Finally, the liberals who had supported the policies of Bismarck at the time of the foundation of the Empire now demanded joint responsibility in the political sphere. They were no longer willing to agree with everything. They opposed, for example, the reduction in the powers of Parliament proposed by Bismarck, and persevered with their demands for a development of the institutions of the Empire along democratic lines. Their policies therefore threatened the authoritarian structure of the Prussian State in Germany, and at the same time the position of Bismarck. The founder of the Empire saw himself increasingly isolated; in internal matters he was embroiled in the struggle between Church and State, and in the sphere of foreign policy his policies were often unpopular. He found himself forced to depend on the co-operation of industry and agriculture.

Indeed, it was this course of action that Bismarck actually took. He dissociated himself step by step from his old adherents, dismissed Delbrück, and systematically destroyed the ministerial basis of the free traders in Prussia. He further encouraged the manufacturers to agitate for protection, and ensured that the economically-based political opposition of the agriculturalists and representatives of heavy industry became entangled with problems of domestic and indirectly also of foreign policy. He used his *rapprochement* with the aims of the protectionists as the excuse for a reorganisation of the Empire. And after 1876, following the formation by industrialists of a new Association (the Central Association of German Industrialists, which was not only successful in conquering the German Handelstag, but was instrumental in preparing an alliance with the agricultural interests), Bismarck used the two attempted assassinations of the Emperor in 1878 as a means of dividing the liberal camp and crushing the socialists. He was also able to cement the alliance between heavy industry, the large banking concerns and the large-scale agricultural producers, which corresponded with the unification of the conservative and centre parties in Parliament.

Repeatedly throughout the course of Prussian and German history in the nineteenth century, an economic settlement between opposing groups had meant the political and social salvation of the feudal aristocracy. This group had succeeded, in the course of the conflict between Austria and Prussia, in integrating the liberals of 1848 within the Prussian state as a state supportive force. Now, in 1879, they cashed in on the commitment of the protectionist opposition (which had found considerable support after 1862, both from Prussia and from Bismarck) as the promoters of their own interests and the guarantors of the system of national protection initiated in 1879. Once again, the degree of solidarity between agriculture and industry in the context of the general protective tariff and the merging of the interests of large landholders, the officer corps, the government bureaucracy and the industrial plutocracy assisted Bismarck's policies and the strengthening of state authority. Even if the general reform of the financial sector did not achieve the aims set out by Bismarck, and the Empire continued to be the poor relation of the individual states, he nevertheless succeeded in splitting the middle class, in crushing the opposition of the fourth estate and in establishing state support from the ultramontanists. As a result, the political balance of power was altered, and the opposition was effectively paralysed.

Those liberal ministers still in office after the first purge were dismissed and replaced by rigorous conservatives. The bureaucratic organisation was restyled according to conservative demands, and the ranks of officials completely purified of free traders. At the same time Bismarck began, albeit unsuccessfully, to replace the Parliament by an Economic Chamber or Privy Council structured along estate lines. He wanted to complete his reform programme with this project and to concentrate the 'social life of the people' in 'corporations and associations under state protection'. The plan failed. But Bismarck could claim at least one success, namely the absorption of the leaders of the economy within the ranks of the Prussian state and its traditional supporters. The upper middle class demanded the possibility of 'rising to the top of the social pyramid' and yearned for 'a style of life which confirmed its membership in the élite' (K. E. Born).

From now on economic, domestic and foreign policy was completely dominated by the unity of interest between agriculture, industry and the leaders of the state. Opposition was prohibited. With the help of protective tariffs, industrial production was to be revived, the price for grain secured and the estate-holders' desire for a stabilisation of the high ground-rents was to be fulfilled.

Thus, the economic reorganisation of the Prusso-German state in 1879 meant a refounding of the state on the basis of principles which were quasi pre-industrial, estate-oriented and autocratic. They involved both loyalty towards and protection of the Crown and the State. Although the ideas of an estate society no longer corresponded with social reality, those groups in the population who effectively ruled Germany, including the industrialists, still thought and lived in the categories of the old estate triad of the nobility, the middle class and the peasantry and added to this system of estates the newly-emergent group of factory workers as the fourth estate (K. E. Born).

Of course the solution that had been achieved in 1879 of domestic, foreign and economic problems would not always heal the latent antithesis between the left and the right, between progress and the restoration of the old order or between liberals and conservatives. This was equally true in the context of the underlying conflict between industry and agriculture, between a mass movement and an élite consciousness and between collective protectionism and a liberal economic system. The world market took no notice of the German 'Union of the strong hand', and even the alliance of large-scale agriculture and a feudalised industrial sector did not prove to be a *unitas sanctorum*.[1] A profound division between agriculture and

1. 'A sacred union'.

industry became noticeable. Industry did indeed benefit from the new constellations, but agriculture increasingly lost its economic significance. This had important consequences. The more these tensions, triggered off by the pseudo-feudal conditions of power and intensified by social problems, were channelled into foreign affairs, the more Germany fell into an isolated position between East and West. The ambivalence of German development led to the dilemma of the conservative system.

6

Stagnation:
*the Dilemma of the Industrialised
Agrarian State*

After the profound political and economic changes of
1879, agricultural prices in Germany stabilised for a time,
and industrial production began the new decade with
increased sales. The great decline appeared to have been
halted. People were convinced, although prices had
occasionally fallen by 50%, that 'thanks to the national
economic policy all sectors of our home industry show
signs of a more hopeful development than they have for
many a long year' (E. Kirdorf). The banks reported 'a sound
situation and substantial activity'. In the mining sector
'the moment did not seem far removed when the consumption capacity of our sales area would reach, if not
exceed, the productive capability of our mines'. In the
chemical industry talk was of an 'almost hectic level of
activity', and this was equally the case in the electrical
engineering industry. Even the textile and handicraft producers hoped for rising sales and full employment at a
time when prices were beginning to recover.

But it quickly became apparent that all these hopes had
been only dreams. The new boom stimulated and organised by the state levelled off surprisingly quickly. Even if
the events of the 1870s were not repeated, the economy
remained characterised until the mid 1890s by an
extremely sluggish growth in the agricultural sector and a

hesitant rate of growth in industrial production as a whole in comparison with the years 1866–72. Equally prominent during this period were a further intensification of the producer goods industries at the direct expense of the consumer goods sector, a considerable fall in the price level of goods in the world market as a result of European industrialisation, a reduction in the rate of return on capital and, connected with this, a diminution in the extent of industrial financing by means of share issues. But this development also took place during a period of a continuously high population growth, accelerating internal migration and emigration, a process of urbanisation which was being accomplished relatively quickly in the key areas of industrial production and a slight rise in wage levels at a time when living costs were falling.

In contrast to the 1870s, therefore, the gains in production and the growth in the economy were not interrupted. However, the movement in price levels particularly after 1857, and their rapid downward decline after 1873, compelled the German economy to rationalise in a dynamic way to keep costs at the lowest possible level and to ensure survival against foreign competition. This led to a considerable change in the proportional representation of different sizes of firms in German industry. Thus the number of concerns in the heavy industry sector was reduced, whereas their productive output and their work-force increased. Medium-sized and small concerns were destroyed by competition or were forced to undertake collective capital investment in order to exploit technological advances. This situation also led to the first wave of amalgamations between concerns in coal-mining, iron and steel production and in the commerical sector in general. The outlines of the first combines and cartels had already begun to appear by the end of the 1870s. Indeed, only specialised firms, particularly in the machine construction sector, were able to retain their position as individual concerns, but these hardly played a major role in the open market or even in the field of technological development.

The key controllers of the process of industrial concen-

74

tration and the 'leaders of the spirit of entrepreneurship' (G. v. Siemens) were the banks. The increased capital requirements of industry strengthened their influence on the development of the economy. They alone were able to overcome the hesitancy and scepticism of the capitalist class in its search for investment opportunities, by acting as agents for debentures and loans to municipal authorities and the state. The banks were thereby able to channel the available liquid capital into industry. As in 1857, this particular crisis also led to an intensification of the relationship between banks and industry, and accelerated the degree of concentration in the banking sector as well as the expansion of large-scale concerns in the industrial sphere. Although taken as a whole the level of investment actually declined, the concentrated application of very substantial funds by the banks enabled a few concerns to utilise technological developments immediately for their own ends. This can be seen in the case of the basic industries, where the Thomas process of steel production was quickly accepted. It was equally true in the context of the electrical industry, where maximum development was now ensured by contracts granted by state and municipal authorities, although this development did not affect the continued control of firms by the private sector. It was also apparent in the chemical industry, where, in contrast to England's, the small-scale, dispersed and dependent concerns were superseded by large-scale firms.

The years 1880–95 were therefore not simply 'an epoch of general discontent' (H. Rosenberg), depression and stagnation. Rather, the basis was laid during this period for the exploitation of new materials and the further development and application of materials already known. New sources of energy were tapped, and existing sources were utilised on a much greater scale. In the fields of advanced mechanisation and the division of labour the emergent large-scale concerns provided an example which could not be overlooked. It was equally impossible to mistake the changes in market conditions, the growth of cities and the advances in science and technology.

Both technical innovations – such as the motor vehicle with its petrol engine, diesel engines, electric lights, power stations, three-phase AC motors, transformers and steam turbines – and organisational changes – such as the emergence of large-scale firms and cartels – cannot be considered in isolation. A decisive aspect of this epoch was the fact that the state administration, despite protective tariffs and the state's supportive measures, (e.g. in the case of the nationalisation of the railway network) failed to initiate a lasting revival of the economy which would, in turn, have produced political stability. The agricultural sector declined further, and its production stagnated. Only by raising agricultural tariffs was it possible to create adequate market outlets for this sector. The trends which had determined the economic upswing in German industry and agriculture alike until this period now took different paths. If harmony had until now been the decisive and characteristic form of development, the feature that was now beginning to emerge proved to be dissonance. The situation, however, was also affected by a second characteristic development of these years.

Even by the end of the 1870s, Germany was still an agricultural state, and the majority of Germans did not live in cities, but on the land. Equally the political views of its citizens were represented within the traditional conservative structure of old Prussia. But by the mid 1890s this situation had changed. Almost 1.5 million Germans had emigrated, and many more than this had found their way from the eastern areas, from East and West Prussia, Pomerania, Posen and Silesia, to the cities and industrial employment, in Berlin, the industrial areas of Central Germany, and finally in the Rhineland and Westphalia. By the early 1890s, industry had achieved a degree of parity with the primary sector as far as the number of people employed was concerned. While in 1882 43.38% of those employed had still worked in agriculture, by 1895 this figure was only 36.19%; an equal number worked in mining and iron and steel production. The agricultural population of Germany had become an urban proletariat and the agricultural state had become an industrial power. The number of employees in the agricultural sector rose by only 0.68% in the 1890s, whereas the increase in industry amounted to 29.4% and in trade and commerce to 48.92%.

Germany thus found itself in the process of becoming an industrial state. Progressive industrialisation had considerably strengthened the position of the entrepreneurs, and their desire to reduce their own costs by dismantling the system of agricultural tariffs had placed the alliance between noble estate and blast furnace under great stress. At the same time, however, migration from the eastern provinces, population shifts, urbanisation and the emergence of industrial centres had further narrowed the basis on which the political power of the conservatives rested. The alliance between the landed aristocracy and the populace began to break up, and as a result, one of the most important pillars which had made possible collaborative political action between the princely houses, the officer hierarchy, the Protestant Church, the bureaucracy and the nobility began to totter. In addition, social tensions had been intensified during the period of economic stagnation, since the state administration knew of no remedy for the problems of the small traders and craftsmen. It was equally impotent in alleviating the threat to the middle class, salaried employees and trade in general, because the state was tied to the interests of big business and large-scale agriculture. It appeared, therefore, that Germany could not take the final step towards industrialisation without at the same time tackling the social problem which accompanied this step. In addition, there was the fact that the socialist and revolutionary opposition parties, despite prohibition, persecution and harsh treatment, had not lost any of their attraction. Work and living conditions were hard, and the consequences of the legislation against the socialists had embittered broad sections of the population. As a result, the antithesis between social classes increased, and class antagonism became more intense. The division within the nation which had been initiated by Bismarck in 1879 now demanded a solution, to overcome the 'economic and social loss of equilibrium' that characterised this 'irritable epoch' (K. Lamprecht).

In the economic and social sphere Germany was unusual, to the extent that despite existing tensions an attempt was made to combine industrial growth with a restorative agricultural policy. There was a distinct hope that the demands of large-scale firms and cartels could be balanced with the policy of internal protection for handicraft production and small-scale concerns. There was a general concern to balance out the claims of landed property, the export and import industries, trade, the wage labourer and the salaried employee – in short, to avoid any extensive reform of the state which would have helped it to adjust to the new social conditions. The crown, the army, the church and the ministerial bureaucracy believed that they were in a position to advance the policy of isolation and integration, either by ignoring the consequences of domestic and foreign policy or by subduing the emergent conflicts of interest through power of the state. But these conflicts were now not simply controversies within the educated middle class, but struggles over economic security and social status. Germany was falling even deeper into almost insoluble dilemmas, namely the antagonisms between agriculture and industry, the haves and have-nots, the small-scale craft producers and the wholesale merchants, salaried employees and wage-earners, the government and parliament and the crown and the people.

The political programme of the agriculturalists during these years was very simple. They fought for the maintenance and extension of agricultural protection, which for the estate-holders was equivalent to the maintenance of their influence in the general administration, politics and the army. They hoped by means of this policy to strengthen the traditional position and power of property ownership and, with the help of their allies, they actually achieved the suppression of liberalism and the stabilisation of grain production on the basis or a roughly static cultivable area. However, they could not prevent the increasing indebtedness on their property, the decline of entrepreneurial initiative and the neglect of technical advance. Protected by custom tariffs which were continuously being raised, the transition to more rational methods of production and adjustments to the demands of the world market could effectively be delayed until a later date. The land-owners used all their energies to preserve the old order, to fight against the mass movement of the lower middle class and the workers as well as against the entrepreneurs and floating capital. But this activity itself led to a change in their relationship with the ruling house and with the state. From a basic 'spiritual tradition' and an underlying philosophy of life, there emerged in the course of this resistance to revolutionary change, international competition and industry a simple ideology of landed property ownership. Prussian conservatism at the beginning of the 1890s simply reflected the programme of 'a mere interest group' (R. Stadelmann) represented by the 'Agrarian League',[1] which itself cemented the alliance between the nobility and the peasantry. Nevertheless it is important to note that although the conservatives were successful in determining the policies of the state under Bismarck, they were able to achieve this only with great difficulty under Caprivi.

The upper middle class, which in 1879 had still voted with the agriculturalists in favour of protection, found itself in an increasingly difficult position in the 1880s, when it became apparent that it was impossible to exclude

1. The 'Bund der Landwirte' (BdL) was created after the Tivoli meeting of the Conservative party (18 February 1893). It supported not only conservative 'Mittelstand' policies, but also high tariffs designed primarily to maintain the economic and social role of the primary sector. With the facade of a new and popular German nationalism, it was able to mobilise substantial sections of peasant proprietors and other middle-class elements within German society, who were united in their opposition to all those forces interested in a new distribution of power within the German Empire. For the 1912 election, for example, the 'Bund der Landwirte' were able to organise about 10,000 political meetings to support their campaign. (cf. D. Stegmann, *Die Erben Bismarcks. Parteien und Verbände in der Spätphase des Wilhelminischen Deutschlands. Sammlungspolitik 1897–1918*, Köln-Berlin: 1970).

English competition by tariffs alone. It was equally apparent that this customs policy effectively provided Germany's trading partners with an excuse to close their own frontiers to German exports. The free exchange of goods had been replaced by a trade war. Russia, which was a market desperately needed by the German export industry, was prepared to open up its markets only in return for a liberalisation of the German agricultural tariffs. But it was becoming increasingly doubtful whether the support of the traditional economic order in Germany really worked to the benefit of the entrepreneurs. However, no matter how great the disagreement among the industrialists, Bismarck and the agriculturalists could always silence demands for a renunciation of the 'alliance of the active forces' by focussing attention on the danger stemming from 'unpatriotic journeymen'. The upper middle class rejected any attempt to reform the political constitution, and was a strict opponent of reform in the sphere of voting rights and of changes in the status quo. Its view of itself as the dominant social class completely corresponded with the ideology of the old estate triad. As the landed, military and administrative aristocracy more than made good the losses which the entrepeneurs had been forced to accept because of the agricultural tariff, the alliance also paid dividends for them. The entrepreneurs benefited from an accelerated policy of ennoblement and armament orders, from the acceptance and encouragement of amalgamation efforts by the large industrial firms (whether in the form of monopoly concerns, cartels or syndicates) and from the nationalisation of public assistance and the railway network. As a result, the cartel of large-scale producers in agriculture and industry retained its viability and thereby allowed Bismarck to implement his policy, even with an insecure majority in the Reichstag. The aim of this policy, however, was to cover the gap between the aristocracy and the feudalised bourgeoisie on the one hand and the common people on the other, by means of a successful colonial policy, an actively-pursued financial policy and finally an energetic social policy.

However, the tensions were reduced only intermittently. The 'economic and social conditions' of Germany still resembled 'a strongly-fired boiler', according to the spokesman of the Ruhr district in both the Associations and Parliament. Neither the active power of the state – which had been strengthened through the reform of 1879 – nor the increasing influence of the ministerial bureaucracy was able to 'lead the dangerously pressurised vapours along channels where they would be able to develop their potential force in a useful way for the individual and as a blessing for the Fatherland'. The newly-acquired territories in Africa probably fascinated a part of the middle class, but the workers proved to be immune to 'the swindle' (as described by Bismarck) which was 'needed only for electoral purposes'. The 'active foreign policy' did not prove to be 'the most successful way of providing a solution to the social question' (G. Henckel v. Donnersmarck), as had been hoped in certain circles. The legislative enactments on medical insurance (1883), accident insurance (1884) and, invalid and old age pensions (1889) were indeed a pioneering achievement, which became a model for many countries, but they failed to produce a reconciliation between the working class and the authorities. According to the judgement of Bismarck and the industrialists, the working class had been led astray by demagogues. The moral conquest of the workers also failed, and they continued to reject subjugation by the state and their naturalisation within the existing national and patriarchal world. What they sought to achieve was precisely what the entrepreneurial class tried to prevent by means of their charitable welfare policies – namely, positive legislation designed to protect workers, a system of work that limited the employment of women and put an end to child labour, protection of wage levels, factory safety and worker participation at a managerial level.

Neither Bismarck, the agriculturalists, nor the entrepreneurs wanted anything to do with these demands. The relatively fast growth in the real purchasing power of wages seemed to them sufficiently adequate social relief. They wanted to secure the traditional order, not to see its dissolution. Their precept for the workers was simply

. . . enjoy what is allotted to you. After you have finished work, remain within your own circles, with your parents, your wife and your children, and reflect on housekeeping and education, This should be your politics and it will give you many happy hours of pleasure. Save yourself the excitement of higher national politics. To occupy oneself with high politics demands more free time and a greater insight into conditions than is granted to the worker. You are doing your duty when you elect recommended individuals through the votes of people you trust. But you can do nothing but harm if you want to seize the rudder of the prescribed social order. Political discussions in the pub are in any case very expensive and you can get much better value at home (Fr. Krupp).

The working class, however, was not satisfied with 'social welfare' 'at home'. Despite legislation against socialists, the Social Democrats gained votes and the working class became increasingly organised and articulate. This was in marked contrast to the liberal middle class, which became visibly divided, in part moving to the right and in part tending towards the left. It sought to preserve its economic and social position in guilds and employer associations, Alternatively, as the educated bourgeoisie it simply appeared as a group of non-organised individuals and therefore very quickly lost its previously dominant role in the party system. The workers recognised themselves as a closed, self-conscious class, and even if their activities were forced into a sub-cultural world the labour question was transformed into a constitutional one, 'which could no longer be solved by means of a purely social policy' (G. A. Ritter). As long as Bismarck's policy of 'national preservation' was supported by the solidarity of interest between industry and agriculture, the labour question — even when viewed as a constitutional problem — could be safely left unattended. Bismarck succeeded in preventing any advance in parliamentary power and in halting any change in economic and social policy by means of alternating coalitions of parties 'concerned with maintaining the state'. The dam which had been created in 1879 against radical change proved high enough to keep back the flood of rising opposition, for the time being.

But as early as 1889, cracks began to appear in the complex structure of the state. The first widespread strike, which destroyed the tentative start of a new upswing in the economy, made clear the extent to which Bismarck's system rested on an unsound basis. When at the beginning of 1890 Bismarck, the agriculturalists and the upper middle class found themselves confronted with a majority in the Reichstag made up of left-wing parties, the cartel collapsed. National liberals and unattached conservatives no longer wanted to follow Bismarck. They not only rejected the cartel, but also dissolved their community of interest with the farmers. As a result Bismarck, who was now determined to solve the 'social question' with a bloodbath, as had been the case in relation to German unification, was deprived of the possibility of a renewed reform of the state from above. The centre found it impossible to initiate a policy of renewed co-operation, and even the young Emperor refused to begin his reign by 'wading in blood'.

Bismarck resigned, but left his successor a bundle of tangled, unresolved and highly explosive problems. In the field of foreign policy there was the treaty with Russia, which even Bismarck regarded as only marginally effective. Further, the alliance system of the Triple Alliance had now been eroded, because of economic and political differences among the signatories. Finally, the agreement with England on the colonial question which had been prepared in 1889 was an issue certain to bring national emotions to the boil in both countries – which it had in fact already done. In the field of domestic politics the outlook was no less hopeless. Financial reform had foundered, just as social policies had failed to achieve the desired effect. Instead, class conflicts had become more intense and the divisions within the nation had deepened. The traditional order appeared to be in extreme danger. In the sphere of economic policy, the system of protective tariffs had led Germany into a cul-de-sac, food prices were high, the market for industrial goods stagnant and the living and housing conditions of the population were wretched and cramped. In Berlin, for example, there were over 20,000 dwellings which consisted simply of one room occupied by eight to ten people.

Faced with such a situation the new Chancellor, Leo von Caprivi, decided to gamble on industrial advance. With the advice of the pupils of Delbrück – and this in itself marked a fundamental change to Bismarck's policies – he decided to rely on a rise in exports. He hoped to revive business activity, which until then had been rather sluggish, by means of long-term trade agreements designed to initiate economic co-operation in Central Europe (M. v. Berchem). He did not intend to maintain the old system of production by means of subventions and political measures, but saw in the opening-up of frontiers and free competition the perfect cure for the symptoms of illness evident in the German economy. However, this also meant lowering agricultural tariffs and hence striking at the roots of aristocratic power and the traditional division of authority in Prussia and Germany.

Caprivi was not frightened of taking this step. He reduced the import tariffs on grain, cattle and wood and used the emergent agricultural crisis of the early 1890s, which forced Germany to depend on imported primary products, to create new market areas for industry, particularly in south-eastern and eastern areas of Europe. In particular, Russia opened up its market, and Germany freed itself from the grips of tariff isolation and began to develop a world-wide trade initiative led by the banking sector. The economy revived and the turn-over of goods rose rapidly.

As a complement to this policy of promoting industry Caprivi, supported by his Minister for Trade, von Berlepsch, began to extend the degree of legal protection for workers. He terminated the persecution of socialists and tried to make good what Bismarck had neglected. In addition, he sought to work with all parties, including the left – which was unheard-of and completely new in Germany. However, with the final ending of the prestigious colonial policy and the reduction of the complicated but ineffective system of alliances built up by Bismarck to a few (as Caprivi hoped) reasonable constellations, a general opposition began to coalesce against his liberal economic policies. The situation was aggravated by his proposed finance reforms, which also affected landed property-owners and were designed to terminate the special rights previously afforded to the middle class. Caprivi had ruined his standing with all existing parties and groups without gaining new allies. He had alienated the agriculturalists because of the reduction in customs tariffs, and had lost the support of the industrialists through his continued policy of protective legislation for workers. Equally, he had alienated the middle class, because he had failed to save them from industrial capitalism, from free competition and from their loss of prestige, both in society and in the state. The support of the officer corps and the Emperor had also been jeopardised because of the reduced expenditure on armaments and the fact that he had vetoed their demands for preventive wars and had implemented reforms in the army. Similarly, the liberal bourgeoisie became disaffected with his conservative policies in relation to education and the Church, and the working class was dissatisfied because, despite all his levelling intentions, Caprivi remained tied to the traditions of a powerful state. As a result, his attempts to solve the problems of an industrialised agrarian state on the basis of enlightened conservatism met with failure. After the energetic revival of the economy, heavy industry once again sought an alliance with agriculture, and with this development the chances of reform were dashed. The legacy of 1879 proved itself to be stronger. It was apparent that liberalism had no roots in Germany.

But the Caprivi interval did not remain without consequence. Henceforward, industry was not a monolithic block, for alongside large-scale basic industries (organised above all in the Central Association of German Industrialists) there emerged a pressure group of those industrialists interested in the acquisition of cheap raw materials and in a reduction in tariffs. This new group constituted a front against the development of syndicates within large-scale industries. Similarly a change also took place in the sphere of the development of political parties and the social order The parties became 'associations for the defence of material interests' (H. Delbrück). The middle class abandoned all political ideas, and from this point onwards concerned itself solely with its own group needs, which frequently found expression in anti-Semitism and ideology. Those groups which at the time of the Empire's foundation had found themselves 'in the final analysis in the same boat' (H. Rosenberg) were finally dispersed into associations of individual economic interests. It would soon become clear whether, in the mid-1890s, a collective policy could solve the inherited and intensified problems of the German nation-state along authoritarian lines, and whether, as at the time of the founding of the Empire, the 'policy of taming' (W. Sauer) could still be successful. Whether or not the German banks and industrialists could retain their position in world markets would also become clear. The ability of Wilhelm II to lead Germany 'towards splendid times' depended entirely on this factor.

7

The Imperial Boom:
the Path to World Economic Power

Germany's population in 1914 amounted to about 68 million. This implied a rise of over 60% in total population since the founding of the Empire. Two-thirds of all Germans now worked and earned their living in the cities — including the 48 large towns which had sprung up – and Berlin, which, with its 3.7 million inhabitants, had left Paris far behind. But the country had not only become the 'most fertile' (C. Fürstenberg) and the 'most populated' (W. Rathenau) state on the Continent; it had also become the 'richest'. Despite the high rate of population growth, German national wealth had increased at an annual rate of 3 to 4 million marks, to over 310 billion marks by the eve of the first World War, as estimated by Karl Helfferich, the director of the German Bank. The German Empire had overtaken England, with its equivalent figure of 300 billion marks, and France, with its 170 billion.

Although these figures tell little about the general prosperity of the nation, the fourteen-fold rise in deposits in savings banks and the doubling of the number of those liable for taxation show that the gains from industrial growth were no longer distributed in an exclusive manner. The hopeless misery which had been all too evident in earlier years now occurred only in rare cases, and despite the continuing destitution of the poorer income groups in the population, there was no unemployment. Production was booming and German imports and exports exceeded those of England, France and indeed even those of the USA. Hamburg's port traffic was surpassed only by that of New York and Antwerp. It is no wonder, therefore, that these years have been described as the 'golden age' and have been judged by academics as the 'golden age of the world economy'.

Germany was not only 'the most populated, richest and most powerful trading' country in Europe, but was also a leading industrial State (W. Rathenau). Stimulated by an extremely favourable economic trend, interrupted by only two short periods when demand levelled off, coal production in Germany had risen by about 290% since the 1880s, which compared well with England's equivalent rise of 80.4%. Germany in 1913 provided almost a quarter of total world production. Pig-iron production increased during the same period by roughly 390% in contrast to a rise of only 13.3% in England, and steel production by about 1,335% as a result of the immediate application of new technological processes. Germany's share in overall world production of these goods rose from 14.6% (1880) to 25.2%, whereas England's share fell from 30.9% to 10.4%. Germany's performance in this sector was bettered only by the United States, whose share of world output in 1913 stood at 42.3%.

In addition to the rise in the coal, iron and steel industries, there were also the achievements of the new branches of industry, which by the end of the 1890s had gradually built up and extended their monopoly organisations. The chemical industry had achieved a prominent position in Europe, with exports from this sector totalling 125 million marks in 1913. Similarly, the electrical industry – with a work force of over 100,000 – had achieved total exports valued at approximately 120 million marks. In less than twenty years Germany had transformed itself from the sales market preferred by English manufacturers into England's sharpest competitor. Germany not only dominated the European market in research and production in the chemical and electrical industries, but had also standardised its industrial production – to a substantial extent in imitation of the North American model. By means of a rationalisation of its organisation, through both horizontal and vertical integration, which became common in the early years of the new century, German industry had achieved a higher performance efficiency than England's, while maintaining lower prices. With the emergence of the problem of market allocation between the competing national economies within a world economic framework, England lost its dominant role precisely on account of its leading technical position of earlier years. Its concerns could not adjust to the rapid changes in the world market, nor satisfy the quick shifts in mass demand. If the high degree of specialisation, the advantages of an island situation and a truly national industrial system had previously been the strength of English industry, it now became clear that these factors were at the same time its weak points. The tradition of the small-scale firm, with its sedate affluence and the consequent extremely loose connections between banks and individual enterprises, prevented a speedy movement towards concentration. In the German economy, the characteristic developments of this period included the rapid utilisation of new materials, the amalgamation of individual firms and the emergence of production organisations which dominated the market. In England, however, the process of concentration in large concerns and the founding of cartels, monopoly organisations and syndicates did not take place, although only by such means would it have been possible to achieve a rapid expansion of firms, increased production, the further division of labour and additional mechanisation. England continued to rely on the 'imperialism of free trade', on its great industrial and economic tradition and on specialised production. Germany, on the other hand, with the help of world-wide sales organisations, extremely close contacts between the banks and industry, and changes in industrial location – as for example in the shift in emphasis from the Ruhr region to the minette ore supplies of Lorraine – sought to strengthen its position and improve its competitive edge. Equally in Germany, purposeful research was energetically pursued and the educational system was reorganised to meet these requirements.

At the same time, however, the changes in the economic structure of Germany during the period were no longer of a fundamental nature. With the protection of Bismarck's customs, sustained by the trade treaties of Caprivi and influenced by the general trend towards conservatism in the political sphere, the development of monopolies and trusts in the chemical industry as well as in the electrical engineering industry was practically complete by the end of the 1890s. The path towards a general system of cartels was finally determined by the founding of syndicates in the heavy industry sector. The new forms of company organisation had also been adopted in the engineering and textile industries, the'processing industry, the building sector, wholesale and retail trade and in the sphere of handicraft production. These organisation structures were in turn reflected in special associations which had in part been founded by the state. The difficulties of adjustment for industry in these areas had been settled by a mixture of liberal, authoritarian and mercantilist measures which were typical of Germany. In this context, nothing changed in the pre-war period.

In terms of decisive innovations, the decade of 'the imperial boom' produced an extension in mass production and the resultant world-wide involvement of German banks and industry. The Berlin banks offered not only an example of concentration and an agglomeration of power within the German economy, but they functioned increasingly as pace-makers for the whole country – now on its way to becoming a world power. In the hands of the Berlin banks rested not only the administration and control of almost 65% of the total indigenous capital of all German credit banks, but also, indirectly, a large part of the work and production procurement for large-scale industry, which had now become the most important element within the Germany economy.

Opportunities for German entrepreneurial initiative appeared to exist everywhere in the world. German consortia and firms participated in the construction of the St.

Gotthard railway, of the Anatolia to Baghdad railway and
railways in Africa and North and South America. They
were equally prominent in similar projects connected
with the founding of mining companies in Africa, Asia,
the Middle East, Russia and France. They helped to found
banks in South America, in the Far East, and ultimately in
Russia, Romania, Turkey, Greece, Bulgaria, Italy, France
and Switzerland. Despite increasing symptoms of weari-
ness in the national market, which became particularly
noticeable during the two crises of 1901 and 1907, the
economic position of Germany in the years following the
turn of the century seemed both brilliant and unclouded.
The image of the German economy was that of a child
bursting with strength, who was well on his way towards
conquering his share of the world.

And yet the German economy did not function entirely
without friction. The negative aspects of the great expansion became increasingly apparent, and began to determine the process of development to an increasing degree.
There had, indeed, been a development of productive
industry on a large scale; and the inner German network of
trade, railway communications and banks had been successfully completed. But despite the fact that the needs of
the population had been secured and the German
economy had finally captured an important part of the
world market, the old problems had still not been solved.
They had merely been covered over by economic growth.
The fact that, despite all efforts, no successful move was
made towards the acquisition of political 'power and
greatness', which in turn had repercussions on the
economy, also meant that traditional tensions inherent
within the political system finally reappeared.

Despite the economic boom, Germany had remained a
country of 'unbalanced growth' (D. S. Landes), with a
divided economic structure. The hope that state tariffs and
other protective measures would revive and stabilise
German agriculture had proved an illusion. Although the
agriculturalists remained an influential pressure group,
agriculture stagnated and failed to be competitive. There
could be no talk of Germany's becoming self-sufficient in

the foodstuffs sector, in view of the rapid growth in population. However, as a result of the imperial policy of autarky, — which met the demands of the agricultural sector — German industry had to suffer once again the increasing opposition of the agricultural nations, particularly of Russia, as had been the case in the 1880s under Bismarck. This time, however, there were serious consequences, because of the steadily increasing demand in Germany for raw materials. The loss of its economic independence was the price that Germany had to pay for its economic advancement. The country became dependent to an even greater degree on world markets. The more the power and volume of Germany's economic production increased, the more its entrepreneurs had to pay increasing attention to competition in world markets, and the more sensitive they became to the limitations of German economic resources. The search for secure sources of raw materials for its indigenous industry came to be regarded as the central problem of national development.

Fear of a social revolutionary movement deterred any tentative acceptance of a free international division of labour as a solution to these problems in Germany. As a result, the imperial policy of national consensus began to receive widespread support, and an attempt was made to make future prosperity and even the country's position as a world power essentially dependent on the extent of its expansion in foreign continents. Increasingly Walter Rathenau's view that 'the peoples of the earth are no longer good friends, but evil competitors' was revived. There was general conviction that only a state that could give battle and win the fight 'for space for its people, space for its interest-bearing capital and space for its most profitable sales' would be able to retain its independence. As 'Germany's power stands or falls with the strength of its industry, it will be "at the mercy of world markets" so long as it does not dispose of adequate sources of raw materials within its own sphere of influence'.

But this policy, which had been initiated in 1897/8 and was regarded as completing Bismarck's efforts to give Germany a world mission, failed. As it was designed to gain for Germany the 'share of world hegemony that was its due' and to 'show the native populations the essence of man and his destiny for higher things' (H. Delbrück), it inevitably resulted in an increasing degree of coalescence among Germany's neighbouring powers. In the face of increased German activity, they set aside their differences. Germany, despite or perhaps because of her substantial successes in the economic sphere, was politically excluded from the circle of the leading powers.

A second no less significant consequence of this policy was that the German banks found that they were forced to restrict their plans and projects. The provision of indigenous capital was too limited simultaneously to finance not only internal expansion and moves towards industrial concentration, and to secure the world-wide trading relations and commitments of both trade and industry, but also to meet the politically-motivated requirements of imperial development aid for Germany's allies. In the sphere of bank politics, developments after 1910 had also led Germany into a cul-de-sac. The consequences were all the more serious as the extensive relocation of German heavy industry in the western provinces had now been completed and the new capacity of the large concerns demanded adequate outlets.

Thirdly, the failure of German international politics also meant the failure of the 'policy of taming' designed to maintain the structure of the state. Even during the period of unfurling imperial power and splendour, integration of the workers within the state had not been accomplished to the extent that the powers supporting the state had desired. On the contrary, the extension in protective legislation for workers, the final abandonment of persecution of socialists towards the end of the 1890s and rising wage levels at a time when the cost of living was falling had produced a division within the working-class movement. These factors had also made it possible for the trade unions, which were in favour of compromise and evolution, to defeat the more radical aims of the Social Democratic Party. But the increasing frequency of strikes – not always supported by the trade unions and the party leadership – indicated just as much as the increasing number of votes for the Social Democrats in the Reichstag elections that the attempted assimilation of the working class in the Prussian state of Germany could not stem from the development of national power without a partial restructuring of the traditional state order.

As a result, the various imperial governments also found themselves in a cul-de-sac as far as this issue was concerned. Their closest collaborators, large-scale industrial and agricultural producers, refused to have anything to do with a policy of social compromise. They wanted to maintain the *status quo* in the context of 'Christian socialism', and demanded 'the overthrow and total destruction of social-democratic trade unions and similar organisations'. They believed, in the words of the General Secretary of the Central Association of German Industrialists, Henry Axel Bueck, that, 'if we achieve this end, we will be praised by future generations as the saviours of the state and society, and as the saviours of a great culture that we can justifiably boast about'.

However, the social basis of this representative body of industrialists and conservatives, which in the economic sense was undoubtedly extremely powerful, became increasingly narrower. The economic upswing, the lack of success in international politics and the attempt at a prudent policy of reconciliation with the left had the effect of strengthening those middle-class, urban, capitalist and industrial forces which did not see their interests effectively preserved in an alliance with the party of aristocrats and feudal agrarians. In particular, the sector of industry dependent on the utilisation of cheap imports tried to force a move to the left and implement a policy of reduced customs tariffs and a general reform of the state. Additional support for these objectives came in part from the chemical and electrical industries, the banks and the progressive liberal parties. As it became clear towards the end of Bülow's era that the vitally necessary fiscal reform was to be carried out at the direct expense of industrialists and floating capital, and would provoke no opposition from heavy-industry, these forces united to find effective organisation and representation in the 'Hansabund'. This collective movement was successful. At the beginning of 1912, together with the Social Democrats, it achieved a significant electoral success over those social groups and parties which had traditionally exercised power. From then on, the deep spiritual division separating the middle class from the feudal aristocracy, and the discrepancy between the economic position of the landed aristocracy and their political claims, could no longer be ignored. The end of the Prussian order in Germany seemed imminent. Germany was isolated in the sphere of foreign policy, having been humiliated in the Morocco crisis, and having quarrelled with England over naval policy and with Russia about the grain tariffs. In the sphere of domestic politics, Germany was torn by insuperable conflicts of interest and threatened both economically and politically by a slackening-off in the boom.

But the representatives of protectionist solidarity did not give up the fight. Indeed, they now began to strengthen their alliance and to make more radical demands. With the slogan that the Empire was now involved 'in a fight for national self-preservation and world acceptance' (K. Helfferich) a new cartel of the 'productive estates' was formed which, despite a declining number of supporters, sought to implement an enormous extension and reform of the armed forces, the safeguarding of the fleet and the promotion of customs tariffs as essential conditions of the 'German system'. At the same time the alliance of conservatives, right-wing liberals, the Agrarian League, the Naval Association, the Central Association of German Industrialists, the 'Wehrverein', the Middle-class Movement and the All-German Federation induced a radical turn in public opinion and forced the government of Bethmann-Hollweg to make equally radical decisions. As far as the nation was concerned, Germany was still the 'strongest military power on the Continent' (W. Rathenau), and the Empire still stood 'strong and proud in glimmering arms' (O. Hintze). But how long could this position be maintained in view of the internal economic difficulties and the problems in foreign policy? How long would it be

The Path to World Economic Power

feasible to cover over the inner conflicts by focussing attention on the drama of foreign events, when foreign isolation served only to intensify internal difficulties? What would happen if German overseas concerns were swallowed up by international consortia? And what should be done if, for example, the German Bank were forced 'to close its doors?' (K. Helfferich)

In order to surmount social tensions, and faced with the necessity of disguising the dilemmas of its system, the imperialist world politics of the German Empire ignored the warnings which the testament of Bismarck provided. Germany, with great ingenuity, pushed its way into the interstices of English, American, French and Russian spheres of interest and played the role of Pericles. It occupied itself with aspects of 'power politics and not with policies which served its own interests' and became increasingly concerned only with national prestige. When this policy eventually failed and proved that it had been pursued by 'a colossus with feet of clay', Germany made a final 'grasp for world power' (F. Fischer), although the path to world-power status now seemed insuperably blocked. Faced with the crisis of July 1914, the German politicians failed to find a diplomatic solution to prevent the outbreak of hostilities.[1] Indeed, it would have been

1. In effect they failed to find another 'Olmütz'. The 'Olmütz' punctation was signed in 1850 by Manteuffel and Schwarzenberg. This related to Prussia's attempt to reform the Germanic Confederation and to extend the sphere of her own political control. It was also linked with the proposals suggested by Radowitz for a smaller Union in Germany, which would enclose all the German states, but significantly exclude both the German and non-German lands of the Habsburg Empire. The immediate conflict which in 1850 seemed to be leading to an outbreak of hostilities between the two main protagonists (Prussia and Austria-Hungary) was resolved on the basis of the punctation, in which Prussia received some small concessions in connection with the Hessian question in return for Austria's consent to a free conference to discuss the reform of the Confederation. Although this conference did in fact meet in Dresden between December 1850 and March 1851, it was a total failure, in that Austria continued to deny Prussia equal status and Prussia in return denied Austria the possibility of including the whole of the Habsburg Empire within the jurisdiction of the Confederation.

difficult to find any solution, since Germany's claim to world power, based on 'the stirring arms of the cyclops' of its industry, had been voiced too often by the most illustrious spokesmen of the nation.

The beginning of the First World War provided the existing economic organisations with a confirmation of their efficiency. They stood the test. But the demand for raw materials immediately became acute, and this problem was to influence the policies of German governments until the end of the war. The efforts of the agricultural sector to achieve self-sufficiency were also now endorsed, as England's entry into the war and the ensuing naval blockade meant that Germany had to depend entirely on its own resources. It became apparent, however, that the concept of autarky, as far as provisions were concerned, would remain an illusion. The longer the population of Germany had to starve, the more severe the situation became. Finally, the outbreak of war also led to the fulfilment of the policy of assimilation. The Social Democrats made no attempt at effective opposition and did not oppose war credits, they remained loyal to the concept of 'a party truce' and marched off to war. Revisionism had fulfilled its purpose.

But state diplomacy, apart from being able to hold Russia up to the German people as the guilty party, was without success, as was shown at the outbreak of war. Germany was surrounded by enemies. The hope of a quick peace proved to be illusory. Nor did the Prusso-German military expertise and barrack-square drill produce a decisive victory. The war became a battle of materials and, despite the victory in the east, ended 'completely other than expected' (William II). The German Empire had come into existence with blood and iron, and in blood and iron it went to its destruction.

During the war, two considerable changes had taken place which affected both the economy, society and the state. Although these changes had their origins in the pre-war period, they were able to develop fully only in the isolated and strained situation of war. These changes, however, were to be of decisive significance for the further development of the German economy.

Although the free market organisations remained largely intact during the war, it soon became apparent that the shortage of economic resources could only be overcome with any degree of effectiveness by state coordination. Indeed, ever since the economic boom of 1879 the influence of the state in the life of the German economy had grown increasingly. The state's intervention had saved a dangerous situation in the case of the nationalisation of the railway network and in the granting of an increasing number of armament contracts for the fleet and the army. The postal services, telephone network, gas, water-works, tramway systems, the Imperial Bank, savings banks and numerous mines were all held by the state on the eve of the war, or were under state or municipal administration and surveillance. This was also true of a multiplicity of large-scale agricultural estates, forests and demesnes. The public component of this mixed economic order, which was typical of Germany, received substantial strengthening through the war. The administration of food supplies brought agricultural production completely under state control, for only by such means would it be possible to regulate and ration consumption. A similar situation came to prevail in the context of government control in the industrial sector.

Already in the first weeks of the war, on the basis of plans formulated by W. Rathenau, 'mixed-ownership' companies were founded on the pre-war model, in which the private sector took over complete control under the overall surveillance of the state. But this element of autonomous administration of industrial production changed as shortages in raw materials became increasingly apparent, and with the occupation and administration of foreign countries by German armies and the continued and intensified nature of the war. Those companies run by entrepreneurs were turned into purely bureaucratic organisations. In 1916, under the shadow of the Hindenburg programme and unrestricted U-boat warfare, compulsory powers over firms and state involvement in private industry received legislative sanction. From then on there was no way of opposing the complete nationalisation of the German economic system. The extraordinary increase in the power of the public sector, and, in parallel, of the bureaucracy, took place largely during the war period. The conflicts to which this situation gave rise were apparent in the peace negotiations at Brest-Litowsk, Bucharest and Berlin, where German entrepreneurs and bankers were able to enunciate their demands and wishes, but where it was equally clear how supreme the administration – and the nature of its concept of the post-war world – had become. It seemed, to the consternation of the private sector, that a decision had been reached in the newly-founded Imperial Agency for Economic Affairs to establish a system of 'German state socialism' with the conclusion of peace. The extension of state powers in the economy was also accompanied by a growth in the power of the trade unions and in particular of the free and social-democratic trade unions. However, the development processes which had been initiated by the war did not only benefit the officials, the military and the authoritarian system of government. Despite the opposition of the entrepreneurs, the trade unions had been able to introduce support benefits for the unemployed, and to establish both arbitration and workers' committees. They had thereby initiated a comprehensive social reform. Co-operation with the state, against which they had previously fought, now paid dividends, as the working class was increasingly valued and recognised as a potent force helping to shape the German political scene. On the other hand, the policy of co-operation adopted by the left-wing parties destroyed their political unity; and the longer the war lasted, the more apparent this became. This in turn made it possible for the old class-dominated state to retain both its power and organisation, as was shown by the delay in electoral reform and the military dictatorship of Ludendorff. At the same time this intensified the workers' hatred for the state, as their plight became increasingly extreme. They were merely the work-force, which not only provided agriculture with preferential treatment, but also facilitated the operation of a black market that benefited the propertied classes. Instead of making peace, the state continued to send German troops in the West and East to their glorious destiny. Patriotism vanished, and there was a general clamour for peace.

After the fall of the Czar in Russia, political feeling also began to ferment in Germany. While the supporters and proponents of a peace commensurate with Germany's position as a world power were once more able to create a unifying centre for their interests in the form of the 'Party of the Fatherland', strikes, unrest, and walkouts began to make clear the extent of the decline in the original spirit of solidarity among the people. Although German troops held and occupied broad stretches of Russia and were capable of initiating a major offensive in the West, Germany was on the brink of collapse. The country's economic and military resources had been exhausted. The state and the country had undertaken too much and had underestimated their opponents. The dream of world power was over.

As the real position of the imperial state became apparent after the failure of the western offensive, it was no longer of avail to attempt immediately to create better conditions for peace by a 'revolution from above', thereby preventing a revolution from below. The concessions came too late. It was impossible to avoid the final outbreak of revolution and the enforced abdication of the Emperor, following the delay in ceasefire negotiations and the general fear of a pointless continuation of the war. Germany was defeated. Although the new state system had still to be inaugurated, it had already become apparent that, even during the war, economic and social developments had essentially followed the same path. The war was over, and the legend of the stab in the back of the fighting armies had been born.

Those parties associated with the maintenance of the traditional state could only view their defeat as a betrayal by the socialists, particularly since considerable trust had just been placed in Hindenburg and the hope of a final victory – despite the fact that the socialists were at that very moment dispelling the phantom of revolution, in conjunction with the army and large-scale industry. A division therefore remained. A break with tradition did not occur even in 1918. But with the attempt to improve the management of Bismarck's inheritance by means of 'a new people's republic' (A. Rosenberg), rather than the bankrupt state of the Emperor, a new era clearly began in German history, at least in the sphere of politics.

8

Prosperity on Credit: Traditionalism in the Republican State

'There can be no second state similar to that of Prussia'. August Bebel had tried to explain with these words the new revisionist direction of the party to the comrades assembled at the party conference at Magdeburg in 1910. He had also stressed that '. . . when we do have that state in our power, then we will have everything'. On 9 November 1918, 'everything' had been achieved. The German Emperor and King of Prussia had abdicated. The fight for a 'place in the sun' had been lost and the 'age of splendour' had given way to the age of blood. But now it became apparent that the Social Democrats had no comprehensive plans which embraced all areas of civil life, particularly the increase in destitution and the problems created by the lost war. They could not provide a compelling alternative to the state with which they had been in conflict for almost 40 years. The Social Democrats, who regarded themselves as 'revolutionaries', were also incapable of ignoring its traditions. Mesmerised by the concept of order of the Prussian state, it was the principal aim of the leaders of the SPD majority who had come to power in the aftermath of the war to restore peace and order, to maintain the traditional forms of national and economic organisations and to secure the continued existence of the state and the Empire. Only with great reluctance and 'at the last possible moment' (G. Kotowski) had the SPD leaders placed themselves at the head of the revolutionary movement: but only after parliamentary reform of the Empire-state had failed. And they did so only to put themselves in a position to immediately block further revolutionary developments.

Already on 10 November 1918, the day after the proclamation of the Republic, Friedrich Ebert – who was seriously afraid of the workers' and soldiers' committees and a potential take-over of power by the independent left – reached a compromise with Wilhelm Groener, the new quartermaster general and Ludendorff's successor. The army declared itself ready to support the new government, and the government, in turn, promised its loyalty to the imperial officers and its preparedness to protect their authoritative powers. As a result, the traditions of the imperial army were preserved despite the military defeat. The attempt to place part of the power in the new state in the hands of the army and the officer corps also succeeded. With this development, 'despite the revolution, the best and strongest element of the old Prussian system was saved and incorporated into the new Germany' (W. Groener).

Alongside this first pillar on which the new state was intended to stand, a second one was erected four days later. The trade unions reached a compromise with the employers in the form of a 'joint association'. As a result any interference by the state in the private organisation of the economy was effectively precluded. 'Let us recognise the trade unions', wrote Hugo Stinnes at the time, 'and grant them regulated working hours, and permit the abolition of restrictions on workers' associations. What we need is a breathing space, which will allow us to get on with our work, and afterwards everything will regulate itself'. Large-scale property ownership remained as untouched as the traditions in the military and economic spheres. Democratic and social reform was deferred for the time being. The new state order was initially restricted to the declaration of unlimited rights of political freedom and social security.

For the majority of Germans the revolution had come to

an end on 10 November 1918. It had impressed the middle class and the nobility that the German people 'had also shown in times of revolution that they had other special characteristics and that they were able to assimilate immediately the unusual events of the revolution because of their positive qualities'. In view of 'Germany's superiority at internal and organised democratisation' and the unbroken effectiveness of the imperial officer corps and state officials, 'the Russian variant of chaos' had no chance of success. What remained was the fear of revolution, particularly among the middle class, and the memory of the lost war, the consequences of which had been placed in the lap of the Social Democrats by those powers which had previously upheld the old state. As a result, the republic, which remained precariously balanced in terms of its very existence until 1924, never had the chance to break the predominant position of the traditional, feudalised upper middle class, the military, the state bureaucracy and the feudal aristocracy, although in the first years of the republic their power still remained veiled.

Despite the abolition of the imperial state and its court and the ending of noble privileges, there was no process of political restructuring, no rigorous elimination of the traditional leading power groups, no revision of the old standards, and no change in the militaristic and authoritarian organisation of firms. There was little nationalisation of key industries; and, where steps were taken in this direction because they had been promised, these were limited either to the creation of self-administrating corporations, as in the potash, coal-mining and steel industries (these corporations were however, very quickly annulled again) or to the nationalisation of public utilities. The railway network became the property of the Empire, and the state and urban authorities finally took over responsibility for the extension of the power supply, as well as for the management of sub-urban traffic, gas, water-works etc.

Despite its self-assertion in the first years and its apparent stabilisation in later years, parliamentary democracy remained merely a disguise for the continued activities of anti-democratic and authoritarian forces which had been able to occupy decisive positions of power in the new state from the very beginning. The mantle of democracy was discarded when it was no longer needed. It was characteristic of this development that the achievements of the Weimar state, including the regulation of the legal relationship between employers and employees, the securing of the position of trade unions, the extension of the possibilities for state intervention in the management of the economy (in particular in the sphere of regulating prices and wages) and finally, the further development of social welfare legislation, all contributed to the accelerated decline in the stability of the state. In the process of the practical implementation of these innovations, the state became increasingly the accountable mediator and fell between the stools of the various interests groups. It became the scapegoat for opposing elements on both right and left, and found increasingly scant support among the political parties. The parliamentary basis capable of supporting the state also collapsed. The more the administration became involved in conflicts over wages and prices and in arguments over the regulation of the economy, the more it lost its power to the extremists. And so it came about that the new state had to operate under continuous stress, not only in the political, but also in the economic sphere; and this dual stress eventually destroyed it.

This development did not simply result from the course of the German Revolution, but was also linked with the peace treaty of Versailles, reparation payments and inflation. All these events weakened the new order of the state and strengthened its opponents. As all invested assets with fixed cash yields, such as state loans, mortgages, debentures and savings account balances, became worthless, so the broad section of the middle class, without whom the new state could not exist, lost their possessions. This led to a situation in which these largely bourgeois groups, who felt their very existence threatened, began to adopt more radical positions and to oppose political changes and the democratic order of 1918, which they assumed to be the cause of all their misery. Attempts on the part of the Social Democrats to seek reconciliation with these groups led to the alienation of the workers; while the latter turned aside disappointed from their previous leaders, the right-wing opponents received continuous new support, owing to post-war developments in the economic sphere. The rapid fall in the value of movable assets improved the relative position of large-scale property owners and strengthened the political influence of the agrarian sector. In addition, the continuous devaluation of the currency enabled German heavy industry, despite the destruction of its raw material base, to reorganise production and to extend the degree of amalgamation in the private sector to an even greater extent than before 1913.

After 1918 Germany enjoyed an industrial boom and full employment, as indeed had been the case during the immediate pre-war period. The post-war fatigue of the world economy did not affect Germany: on the contrary, it only served to increase German sales.

But this boom was an artificial blossoming, an inflationary boom financed by extensive short-term bank credits, which could be employed for long-term investments because their repayment had been made superfluous by devaluation. Whereas the Reichsbank calculated a devaluation premium of 25% to 85%, the actual devaluation quota in 1922, for example, stood at 3,000% and over one million per cent and one billion per cent in 1923. The loss in value had finally become so substantial that money could no longer play a role in the economic life of Germany. Germany returned to a system of barter trade, and in the process of this transition it became clear that 'the industrial boom had been largely fostered by the disappearance of actual capital' (G. Stolper).

Germany had not been able to make good the loss of 74.5% of its iron ore supplies, 68.1% of its zinc ore, 26% of its coal production, its potash monopoly, its navy and a large part of its mercantile marine. Despite feverish activity and a high level of exports, the loss of patents, foreign capital investments and the transformation of the Alsace textile industry into one of its most bitter competitors, proved too much. Directly after the war the excess in purchasing power had led to inflation; and since Germany found itself increasingly dependent on imports, whereas its own exports were calculated as part of reparation payments (the level of which had not yet been established), prices began to rise. At the same time confidence began to collapse and the circulation velocity of the mark began to increase. Reparations and compensation for 'all damage caused by German attacks to the civil population of the allies and their property, whether on land, at sea or in the air' had been fixed at such an extraordinarily high level at the peace negotiations that, had Germany ever been able to realise these demands, it would immediately have become the unpaid provider for the whole world.

Reparations, therefore, made the German position increasingly hopeless, and in the final analysis, contributed significantly to the process of political radicalism. They also accelerated the decrease in value of the German currency, which had been started by the methods used to finance the war and was aggravated by the terms of peace and the means by which Germany raised credit and currency. The problem of reparations finally led to the myth of the conquering Allies and the vanquished Germans, culminating in the 'battle for the Ruhr' which ultimately pushed the country into catastrophe. But despite the hardship caused by the occupation of the Ruhr by Belgian and French troops, the conflicts of 1923 did produce something positive, namely a basic and not merely organisational reform of the German currency and the financial system. The problem of regulating reparation payments could, however, no longer be deferred, as the policy of increasing the monetary supply had now begun to affect landed property and industrial production.

On 15 November 1923, shortly after the 'battle for the Ruhr' had been suspended, the first step was taken. A billion marks became one gold mark. This succeeded in creating confidence in the new currency and obviated the need for a repeated increase in credit. The rate of exchange stabilised. But this alone did not put an end to all existing problems. Although industry had been freed from indebtedness by the effect of inflation, new working capital for the continuation of business was still lacking. Under these conditions, only regulation of reparations on an international level could provide any assistance. America had a primary interest 'in restoring to Germany its functional ability in world markets, continuing the international division of labour, and thereby raising world-wide productivity' (W. Fischer). Only when that country which had to meet the largest number of payments could dispose of part of those payments in the form of credits would it be possible to equalise the balance of payments discrepancies.

Germany was therefore granted a breathing-space in its reparation payments under the terms of the Dawes plan. At the same time, the amount of the instalments and the timing of the payments were also fixed, as well as the sources from which they were to come. After the acceptance of this plan, a period of recovery began for Germany and its economy 'the extent and dynamism of which had not been previously rivalled in the history of Germany' (G. Stolper).

Production was now rationalised according to the American example in order to meet the demands of a highly organised capitalist economic system. And with the help of foreign capital, which sought an area of investment in Germany after the process of stabilisation, new and replacement investment could be implemented on a wide scale from indigenous capital resources. Germany was also able to take part in the economic application of technical advances, particularly in car and aeroplane construction, films, radio and artificial silk. The electrical engineering, chemical and optical industries were once more able to establish leading positions in world markets. Production was also increased in machine construction, in the textile industry, in the mining sector and in the steel industry – although no longer stimulated by the apparent advantages created by inflation. The increase was both considerable and constant. Salaries and wages achieved their pre-war level, and by 1927 the industrial production of the Republic had already exceeded that of the Empire. The export of goods was 7% above the level of the year 1913, and the number of unemployed had reached its lowest level for the 1920s.

Parallel to this economic upswing, which was significantly supplemented by the granting of contracts for building projects by the central government, the regional states and local authorities, there was a new movement towards concentration in German industry which finally brought to a close the pre-war trend. From a total of 20 billion RM share capital, which represented the interests of over 12,000 limited companies, 13·25 billion marks were allotted to a mere 2,000 companies. 93% of the mining sector, 96% of the chemical industry, 95% of the steel industry and 87% of the electrical engineering industry were organised in combines, cartels or trusts. Despite the burden of reparation payments, foreign indebtedness, the oscillating parliamentary majorities and violent political disputes, the country gradually recovered.

At the same time these years of stabilisation and stability during the Weimar republic were characterised by a different situation as compared with the pre-war period. The inflationary boom must be measured by other criteria than those which are applied to world economic growth. The upswing after 1924, at least in Germany, was far more a mixed boom than a balanced growth, based on an effective reorganisation of economic conditions. Production began to stagnate as early as 1927. The enormous and often over-hasty expansion financed by expensive credit was followed by an excessive burdening of the economy with debts and interest payments which adversely influenced the competitive position of German firms. As wages had been kept stable by the state administration because of their political character, and prices were strictly controlled by the agreements of cartels and syndicates, production had to be cut back. Indeed, even during the period of expansion only 50 to 70% of productive capacity had been used. Only through an increase in state ownership of the means of production, through state activity as a banking agency and overall state intervention, had it been possible, in collaboration with syndicates and monopoly concerns, to avoid a continuous fluctuation in the indices, at least in relation to the capital goods industries. But this co-operation was increasingly threatened as economic growth was accompanied by wage disputes and the burden of interest payments. As a consequence of state commitments and monopolistic agreements, however, it had not been possible to bring the rigid price agreements into line with the economic development of a free capitalist society. German industry could not free itself from the burdens and consequences of the war.

This was particularly apparent in relation to the large Berlin banks, which had once again become the arbiters of free play among entrepreneurial forces, even if the game had now been limited by monopolistic agreements and the existence of state concerns. But the banks, nevertheless, failed to enjoy that degree of sovereignty which they had exercised in the pre-war period. Their financial capital had largely been destroyed by the end of the inflation period, and with 'a capital stock that had shrunk to one-fifth of its pre-war level' (K. E. Born), the large requirements of industry could simply not be met. As a result, so long as capital accumulation in Germany was only now beginning to revive, the only alternative left was to secure finance from abroad, in particular from those countries to which Germany had to render the high yearly payments of reparations. The Dawes plan now helped to solve this contradiction – on the one hand reparations obligations, and on the other hand the need for loans. It enabled the use of foreign credit, not only for stabilisation purposes and to enable Germany to make a new start, but also for the payment of reparation debts. The shortage of indigenous capital stock could not, however, be compensated for by these short-term credits. The liquidity position of the banks, and therefore of the economy as a whole, remained visibly weak. Although it was stressed time and again that, in view of the high degree of German participation in the investments begin undertaken, there could be no talk of a boom supported from abroad (G. Kroll), the German economy was still dependent on foreign countries, as was demonstrated by the development of the world economy during these years and the balances of individual banks and firms. It was, therefore, threatened both by the need for security on the part of overseas providers of credit and by the burden of reparations.

The development of the economic boom was accordingly unsettled. In addition, it became increasingly dependent on the directive role of the state machine, which saw itself compelled to interfere in the running of the economy on a continuous basis, simply because of the unbalanced nature of economic growth. This meant that expansion and stability, despite all internal efforts, reflected a borrowed prosperity that could not and did not correspond with the ultimate security of the nation. The defeat could not be simply paid off. In addition, towards the end of the 1920s, Germany paid the price for its failure to implement agricultural reform. Agriculture became again the complaining lodger of the economy, in need of further protection and thereby encroaching on the freedom of decision-making available to the republican state.

The limited stability of economic development in Germany after 1924 became apparent as a general downswing in the world economy towards the end of 1928 led to the stagnation of sales in the consumer industries. At the same time a world-wide fall in agricultural prices made an extensive and expensive system of protective measures vitally necessary for large-scale property owners in Germany. The post-war boom and speculation fever in America also collapsed into a crisis, which led to a shrinkage in world trade on a scale previously unheard of in the whole history of the world economy. 'A happy and wild noise had filled the earth during the period of upswing. Now uneasiness settled over the world' (A. Döblin). The continent of Europe, particularly Austria and Germany, had no powers of resistance to set against the recession. They were drawn for the third time into the whirlpool of a world-wide crisis.

The 'chain links in the fabric of the German economy' (G. Stolper) had broken. Between 1929 and 1933 exports collapsed from 13.6 to 4.9 billion RM, although every third industrial worker in Germany was dependent for his livelihood on this sector. At the same time imports were cut back. Between 1929 and 1931 the national wealth of Germany (GNP) fell from 75.9 to 57.5 million RM and German industrial production also fell by 33.7%. The result was massive unemployment, which quickly became a permanent feature, as Brüning's government, fearful of a new inflationary situation and following contemporary economic theories, tried to maintain the exchange rate. This involved a strongly deflationary policy and the application of political pressure to bring down home prices and thereby to compensate for the price falls in important competitor countries which had traditionally been good markets for German goods. But the government's measures failed to overcome the crisis. Despite the problems in agriculture, trade and industry – as well as in the banking sector – the experiment would probably have succeeded in restoring stability to the German economy (by means of reductions in public spending, increased taxation, reductions in salaries and wages, moratoria and exchange controls) if it had not been for one factor. The unexpectedly heavy and rapid fall in production and income, the rise in the number of unemployed in the years 1931–3 to over 6 million, the complete collapse of the stock market, with the average share value falling from 148 in 1929 (1924/26 = 100) to 54 by 1932, all had serious political ramifications. This was equally the case in relation to the destruction of property values through bankruptcies, arbitration proceedings and forced sales.

During the course of the crisis it became apparent that economic stability had not been achieved in Germany in the post-war period. Furthermore political stability was still lacking. The pressures of economic disaster paralysed not only the cycle of economic activity, but also the democratic and republican exchange of interests and opinions. Indeed, the beginning of the economic crisis had already led to a government crisis in 1927 over the problems of provisions for the unemployed, which on the face of it seemed to have been solved. The later attempts designed to overcome social, economic and political difficulties without recourse to Parliament, by means of emergency decrees, only led the country even deeper into the dilemma. The crisis of government became a crisis of the state, which helped reactionary forces to break through and ruined the efforts of the liberals and democrats. Under the protective umbrella of the unity of interest between large-scale agriculture and industry, the conservative administrative bureaucracy, and the imperial army, a move was made towards the right and the way smoothed for dictatorship. The Weimar state had failed to solve the German dilemma. In its collapse it revealed the inherited conflict of interest, which had now gone through a process of extreme radicalisation. Once again, as had been the case in the days of the Empire, national collectiveness seemed to be the only way out of the economic and political crisis for the majority of Germans, a view that was reflected not simply in the votes cast for the NSDAP.

9

The Dictated Advance:
the Transition to Blood and Iron

The inheritance which the Weimar state left to its successor can be roughly sketched out in the economic and social field under four headings.

(1) The crisis, if not yet surmounted, was at least halted and in the process of subsiding. Despite the continued misery of unemployment, poor credit provision and empty order-books in industry, this development was clearly reflected in the level of stock exchange values and the rising prices of raw materials. This had been achieved with the help of deflationary policies, American aid and a general extension in credit provisions.

(2) The crisis in the banking sector had put an end to the payment of reparations, and with the Young plan a return to economic and financial autonomy had been made possible.

(3) Because of the extent of indebtedness and the catastrophic business position, the great private credit banks, in particular, had been forced to agree to an economic structure which came very close to being a developed form of state socialism.

(4) The Junkers, large-scale industry, and the higher ministerial bureaucracy had all preserved their influence. None of the alternative political groups which had emerged during the crisis period and at the beginning of

114

the 1930s regarded a return to the free market economy as possible or even desirable. As a result of the crisis, the model of an economy organised according to liberal principles – if this had ever been still operative in Germany after the year 1893 – had finally disappeared. There was no opposition to an all-powerful state presence in the economic field. On the contrary, the great majority of Germans wanted the economy to be organised by the state and hoped thereby to achieve an improvement in their position. This was equally true of officials and salaried employees, as well as workers and self-employed craftsmen. Inflation had destroyed all their savings, and in the ensuing period of expansion they had not benefited from the abundance of credit that had been distributed by a very small group to an equally small segment of society. It now became apparent to these groups that the worker had to sell his labour and that craftsmen and small-scale firms had been overwhelmed by large concerns. It was equally clear that the same process had occurred in other sectors, with the small business being replaced by the department store and the farmer giving way to the tradesman. But whereas the workers, in collaboration with left-wing parties, hoped to make good the lost opportunity for revolution which had been wasted in 1918, the threatened middle class put all its hopes behind a radical national revival, in accordance with tradition.

The boom initiated by the National Socialist state was therefore able to depend on a number of factors, including a professional administrative apparatus dedicated to its national goals. It could also count on the willingness of the people to recognise those values which were almost obligatory for Germans, such as 'discipline, duty, virtue, obedience, a reliance on authoritarian leadership, national greatness, the subordination of the individual and the "total unity" represented by the state' (R. Dahrendorf). In addition, it could build on the foundations of an economic order in which the state already exercised command over the banking mechanism, exerted full control over the money supply and had occupied the most important command posts in the economy, including the transport system, the fuel supply and the regulation of cartel prices (G. Stolper). The reorganised system of taxation, customs dues and social insurance contributions, and the extremely high degree of state control over the means of production, provided the state with about a 50% revenue share in the country's gross national product.

This was the basis on which the NSDAP was able to develop its economic policy. That policy, however, never constituted a carefully thought-out programme, but rather emanated from tactical party considerations during the Weimar period. The defined goals and guidelines set out in their party programme, including 'the commonweal before self-interest', 'the breaking of the bonds of interest slavery', 'land reform', 'the communalisation of department stores' and the 'nationalisation of all incorporated companies', were, however, never realised. Only those forms of organisation which had been tried out during the First World War were actually employed. Supported by highly skilful propaganda, which utilised the traditional animosity of the middle class (in particular of the lower middle class) against liquid capital, as well as against the prospect of a Red revolution, which had been intensified during the crisis, the NSDAP succeeded in reducing decisively the problem of mass unemployment in a fairly short time. It was supported by its allies, namely the interest groups of conservative agriculturalists and the industrial upper middle class. The reduction was effected by means of state work-creation policies, a very risky policy of exchange creation which skilfully avoided a devaluation of the currency, high agricultural tariffs and a strictly protectionist-orientated foreign trading policy. Industrial production was again stimulated, modernization of industrial plant was begun and agricultural reforms were introduced designed to organise the primary sector as a compulsory cartel in the Reich's Food Estate. The NSDAP thereby effectively controlled and co-ordinated both cultivation and marketing, and sought to achieve a price structure independent of world markets. It also aimed at achieving German self-sufficiency.

As it had promised, it succeeded in creating employment and securing the people's livelihood. The increase in money supply, the promotion of house construction and the erection of magnificent public buildings, road construction, land improvements, and the establishment of airports, defence dispositions and barracks proved to be extraordinarily successful policies, particularly in the light of the inflation and economic crisis of the Weimar period. They also made good propaganda: the more negative attendant symptoms of the first Four-Year Plan, which to a large degree represented simply a modified continuation of the policies of Weimar, as in the field of foreign policy, could effectively be concealed. Without completely destroying the external form of the capitalist structure of the German economy, the right wing of the party under Adolf Hitler, with the support of the military and the representatives of heavy industry, was able to organise the economic, social and state structure of Germany according to the Nazi 'principles of leadership'. It had been equally unnecessary to nationalise private concerns, as the party programme had anticipated, and in fact those concerns which had fallen into the control of the state during the crisis period were even returned into the hands of the private sector. The opposition elements within the party which wanted to see the 'national revolution' followed by a 'social revolution' were liquidated. Parties, trade unions and interest groups were disbanded and transformed into regionally-organised national branch associations tied to the Party. The NSDAP also succeeded without difficulty in integrating the activity of entrepreneurs in the private sector within a state-controlled system of contracts and marketing, which increasingly took over the function, formerly exercised by the market mechanism, of balancing supply and demand, the exchange of goods and settlement payments.

But already by the end of the first Four-Year Plan it had become apparent that the solution of unemployment problems and of the crisis in general on the basis of a closed and centrally-administered economy also created additional problems which could not be dealt with within the context of a hazy ideology of a corporative estate structure.

The Transition to Blood and Iron

Although state dominance of production, distribution and consumption had been assured, the results of an all-pervasive surveillance and nationalisation of the German economy were not only a crippling of private initiative, but also economic isolation, contraction in the market, increasing scarcity of indigenous resources and, as a concomitant, increasing indebtedness. Economic management of all business activity had now become essential. The type and quantity of production, estimates, profit margins and sales had to be controlled and organised on an increasingly rigid basis. Such a policy, however, failed to make clear how further economic expansion – which was and ought to have been based purely on the utilisation of indigenous resources – could in fact be achieved by these methods. Financed by a system of credit creation (Mefo bills) which was without doubt ingenious but also precarious, and which involved the investment on a long-term basis of the 'short-term cash supplies which the market was able to make available' (H. Schacht), the outlook for the economic upswing was not favourable. Deprived of export opportunities as well as the possibility of imports, without foreign credit and currency, and tied to the political programme of autarky and national rearmament, the boom was bound to change abruptly into inflation and stagnation – at the very latest when, at the start of repayment, no cover would be available. This was particularly true in the case of Hitler's Empire, since the cover consisted of, and was intended to consist of, a military arsenal and military successes.

This juncture was reached by 1936. The process of recovery from the crisis had been completed. The producer and consumer goods industries had recovered, the standard of living had reached approximately the 1928 level, and the German people now had to enjoy 'the honour of work', 'the beauty of work' and 'strength through joy'.[1] No budgetary plans and no statements con-

1. These activities represented integral aspects of the propaganda work of the Nazi Labour Front. Apart from the 'Honour of Work', the 'Beauty of Work', as a division of the Labour Front was to deal with such questions as the improvement of ventilation and lighting

118

cerning the Empire's indebtedness were published from the beginning of 1936 onwards. The amount of Mefo bills in circulation rose to over 40 billion RM, without effective cover. It was now increasingly apparent that devaluation of the German currency could be prevented only by a wage and price freeze. Even the expropriation of Jewish property and the cancellation of foreign debts could not ameliorate the situation. Despite the semblance of power both internally and abroad, and the resplendent development of the 'Führer' state, the whole system was threatened by financial and economic exhaustion and stagnation. In this situation, the regime decided on a solution of the financial problem by military rather than economic means.

The second Four-Year Plan finally linked together economic development and rearmament, without any attempt at concealment. The armed services now became the central point of the state's interest. In the field of foreign policy, as in the case of domestic, economic and financial policies, apparent peaceableness was now jettisoned in favour of unconcealed aggression and a fantastic search for prestige by means of brutal oppression. The German economy was intended to become self-sufficient and, like the German army, to be ready for war in four years. There was now no foreseeable end to the process of rearmament, and there could no longer be any concern for profit calculations by accountants. From now on it was to be a question of 'victory or destruction' and the game was to be played 'for the highest stakes' (H. Göring). Moreover, there was no trace of opposition. The prospect, on the one hand, of a fall in living standards and an enforced restriction of births, and, on the other hand, the existence of large military forces and the need to secure their maintenance, left Adolf Hitler, according to the tes-

in factories, the installation of rest rooms and the general improvement in working conditions. The 'Strength through Joy' organisation, on the other hand, was primarily concerned with the collective organisation of the leisure activities of the German people, and provided a wide range of different activities, including vacation travel, theatre performances, courses in gymnastics etc.

timony of the Hossbach protocol, 'with no other alternative but action'. It was therefore decided that the question of additional territory for Germany would have to be resolved at the latest by 1943/5. To achieve this programme, agriculture, the banks, trade and industry all had to make their contribution, without any consideration of the actual cost. 'I demand', ordered Göring on 7 December 1936, 'that you do your utmost and provide proof that part of the nation's wealth has been entrusted to you'.

As a result agriculture and industry did everything to produce the required proof. Agricultural production increased to the extent that Germany could meet almost 80% of its requirements. Production for rearmament by German industry achieved record figures. The quantity and quality of substitute materials were substantially raised, despite heavy initial costs. Under the pressure of the enforced need for self-sufficiency, German industry achieved a position of leadership in the field of technological research. Artificial silk, acetate, artificial rubber and substitute fuel replaced the natural raw materials which, although substantially cheaper, still came from abroad. Rearmament was therefore able to continue, despite the bottlenecks and restrictions which the increasing level of economic isolation produced. But self-sufficiency was not to be completely achieved. Germany remained dependent on foreign supplies of fats and meat products; this was equally the case for iron ore, copper, zinc, manganese, chromium, tungsten nickel, raw textile materials, skins, petrol and mineral oils.

Instead of leading to economic self-sufficiency, the Nazi policy led to a general impoverishment, since although unproductive rearmament expenditure guaranteed full employment, it also ate away at the standard of living. Behind the apparent trend towards 'a steadily rising national income', there existed 'an actual increase in the level of impoverishment' (F. Lütge). Inevitably, in 1939, after the Mefo bills due for redemption had been incorporated into the 'quite montrous' overall debt of the Empire, the printing presses began to turn again (H. Schacht). The time had come when the promises of the

National Socialists would have to be redeemed. The leadership believed that the problem of living space, related to the problem of maintaining industrial production and life, could be solved only by means of war and a renewed attempt to seize world power. Only 20 years after the first catastrophe, Hitler unleashed the Second World War. Equipped with a hard-hitting army and an efficient industrial structure, he hoped to obtain by force the 'guarantees and sureties' for Germany's position as a world power. But once again, Germany overestimated its chances and underestimated its opponents. Hitler believed that he would be able to defeat the superior forces of the enemy in a short war, without having to prepare the German economy for a long struggle and total war. He reckoned with a quick victory, and thought that the expected reparation payments would cover all expenditures. Half the necessary financial requirements, for example, remained uncovered, and even until 1942 work proceeded on a peace-time basis. Civil consumption remained relatively high. Quick initial victories and breathtaking successes seemed to justify Hitler's suppositions. The ore of France, the oil of Romania and the coal and wood of Poland, and later the riches of Russia, effectively supplemented the industrial potential of Germany, Austria and Czechoslovakia.

Only as the war began to last longer than expected, as the ring of enemy powers became tighter, and the first lightning successes were halted by the unexpectedly tenacious opposition in the East and in England, was a start made on centralising the economy. From this point onwards, military and civil requirements were planned precisely. German industrial production reached its peak in the last years of the war, at a time when Germany was completely cut off from the outer world, during the phase of total war and the great battles of men and materials. Only with the loss of those industrial areas occupied and exploited by Germany, in particular in France and Belgium, and with the destruction of industrial plant and the transport network in the Empire itself, did the armaments industry suffer any considerable setback. Indeed the large concerns in the heavy industry sector, in mining and in the chemical industry, although affected by cuts and losses, were still able to continue functioning until the capitulation. In the spring of 1945 the German economy finally received the decisive blow. As a result of active fighting on German soil and the gradual occupation of the Empire, the transport network became unserviceable and industrial plants were either destroyed or abandoned. Unspeakable chaos, want, suffering and despair broke over the country. The war which German troops had successfully carried into other countries now surged back towards Germany, and in this flood the Third Empire which was to have lasted for 1,000 years, collapsed after only twelve, and capitulated.

In contrast to its condition after the first catastrophe of 1918, Germany was now completely ruined. Its army could no longer return home unmolested. Its economy had not only been ground down, but had been completely extinguished. No revolution could set in motion a process of political renewal. The victors occupied the country and Germany was now without any political identity, a nation without a state. Its industrial concerns and its transport networks had been destroyed, its cities had been bombed out, and its people lived as before in fear and destitution. They were in the process of migrating from the eastern to the western provinces, in search of food, places to stay, and their next of kin. Total defeat followed total war and gave way to hatred and scorn. By the end of the war the Allies were unanimous amongst themselves: 'there's no good German but a dead German'.

10

The Divided Economy:
the Fruits of Defeat

At their great conferences during the War the Allies achieved unanimity: on the one hand, they would not be able to occupy Germany indefinitely; on the other hand, they were convinced of the necessity of controlling with exact precision the reconstruction of Germany's social, economic and political life, in order to prevent the defeated power from ever again being in a position to start a war. From 1941/2 onwards there were a multiplicity of different plans in existence concerning post-war Germany and the form in which it should be allowed to re-emerge. These ranged from its dismemberment to its complete de-industrialisation and restructuring as an entirely agrarian state. In the words of Morgenthau, 'Germany's path to peace progresses by way of the peasant homestead'. However, the agreements of Yalta and Potsdam embodied the decision that, although Germany was to be allowed to remain unified, 'the Germany economy was to be decentralised in the shortest possible time, with the aim of destroying the existing excessive concentration of economic power represented in particular by the cartels, syndicates, trusts and other monopoly organisations'. This decision was to be implemented after the final severance from Germany of those areas east of the Oder-Neisse, which was to be regulated in the peace treaty. All 'production of metals and chemicals, machine construction and the manufacture of other articles directly necessary for a war economy' were to be controlled and limited according to the Potsdam agreement. According to this principle, as indicated in the regulations attached to the so-called industrial plan of 1946, the capacity of the steel industry, for example, was to be reduced to about 25% of the production figure for 1938. For other industries the comparative figure was fixed at 32% for the basic chemical industries, 53% for the cement industry, 55% for the textile industry, 11.4% for the machine tool industry and 31% for the heavy machine construction industry. Plant for the production of so-called armaments manufacture was to be completely prohibited and dismantled and this was to include arms, ammunition, war equipment, ballbearings, roller bearings, tapered roller bearings, tractors, petrol, oil, rubber, ammonia, ocean-going ships, planes, raw aluminium, magnesium and wireless equipment. Only the coal-mining sector was to be allowed to flourish in the interests of the Allies, but its prosperity did not benefit the German economy. Reduced to 'a state of poverty' (K. Borchardt), the defeated and dismantled country continued to vegetate after 1945, with an industrial production as planned by the Allies equivalent to only 30–40% of the 1936 figure, and without a fleet or an air force, exchange of goods or any market organisation.

Hatred for Germany was a general phenomenon. Germany remained a country without an effective head, occupied and divided into four sectors. In future its finances, transport system, foreign trade and industry were to be controlled. It was intended that the German economy should undergo a fundamental change. Surpluses were to be allowed only in those goods suitable for reparations payments, in order to compensate to the greatest possible extent for the loss and suffering which had been inflicted on the Allied nations. The German people could not be absolved from full responsibility for those losses. The victors were united in the punishment and persecution of Nazism, which involved the confiscation of the fleet and of overseas property, the dismantling of industrial plant and extensive reparations payments. By these means it was intended to keep German industrial production within bounds. Indeed under the influence of the recent and horrific experiences of war the Allies were able to achieve a general understanding on this programme. But they were not able to reach agreement on a common policy that would extend to the destruction of Germany's glory and splendour, particularly as the image of war and its suffering increasingly faded and the plight of the German people grew. At this juncture, with the absolute defeat of Hitler's Germany and the spirit of Nazism achieved, the sole common interest which had compelled the two fundamentally different social systems, represented among the Allies to co-operate effectively disappeared. The fundamental antithesis between the two systems – on the one hand the capitalist monopoly economy and the presidential democratic form of the state, and on the other hand the socialist-planned economy and the people's democracy controlled by the party – once again came increasingly to influence world politics and therefore the development of Germany.

Already in Potsdam the first conflicts had emerged between East and West, and they appeared equally insuperable in the Control Counsel for Germany which was set up on 30 August 1945. Stalin, as it became apparent, had a hard and fast concept of his political aims. Whereas Roosevelt lent all his dying vitality to the problem of securing world peace and hoped to regulate European problems through the mechanism of a general organisation for world peace, Stalin concentrated completely on cultivating Soviet influence in eastern and central Europe and utilised the power vacuum which had been created by the advance of the Red Army for the aims of Soviet politics.

While Germany everywhere still lay in ruins, without a functioning railway system, postal service or telephone network, and when improvisation was the motto of the day, the groundwork for later development was laid in the Soviet-occupied zone by cadres of trustworthy functionaries who had been trained in Russia. In the Autumn of 1945 the democratic reform of the land was implemented and large-scale landholders were deprived of their property. This marked the beginning of a clear-cut and radical policy of socialisation, which was designed to destroy the basis of the agriculturalists' party interest and which had already been initiated through the amputation of Pomerania, East Prussia and Silesia. It was also designed to delineate clearly the break with German tradition. At the same time further steps were taken to abolish the private capitalist economic system; this was easily achieved since most big industrialists and large-scale landholders had emigrated to the West following the occupation of this area by the Red Army. Those who still remained were probably only too willing to co-operate with the Soviets and their allies.

In the autumn of 1945, Chambers of Industry and Commerce were established according to socialist principles, which meant that the participation of entrepreneurs was precluded. Economic boards were founded as internal organs of the party, to work out the economic plan of 1946 and the future organisation of a planned economy. Bit by bit the Soviets, who had borne the brunt of the fighting during the war, dismantled and reorganised the areas which they occupied. They extorted reparations payments which they had fixed at Potsdam at 10 billion dollars, and continued to cling to their zone, when their previous Allies had given up the idea of a common policy for dismantling plant and reparations payments. The amazing thing was that the revitalisation of the economy in this area, despite the comprehensive, uncontrolled and often senseless and unplanned process of dismantling which was in part implemented on numerous separate occasions, was even more remarkable than in the zones occupied by the Western powers. Any continuation of the traditional structure of production, or even a renewal of the capitalist system, was, however, hardly conceivable. In the first place, a large number of the most important concerns in the coal-mining, iron ore and potash sectors, and in the sphere of fuel and electricity production, had been confiscated. This was also the case in the metal, engineering and electrical industries, in the precision engineering, optical, chemical

and cement industries, and in car production, as well as in
other branches of industry. Secondly, these concerns,
worked solely for the USSR as so-called Soviet joint-stock
companies until the 1950s. Equally in the sphere of industrial organisation, the end of the war brought about a profound turning-point and led to a total restructuring, which
corresponded with similar changes of a fundamental nature
in the social and political fields.

The Soviets had already succeeded by the spring of 1946
in forging the recently revived political parties and trade
union organisations into a union of socialists and com-
munists within the SED. Indeed, immediately after the end
of the war they had authorised at the lowest level a controlled and democratically organised administration.
When, a few months later, the expropriation of all entrepreneurs listed as Nazis and war criminals was initiated
on the basis of the public referendum of 30 June 1946 in
Saxony, the future of this part of Germany had to a large
extent already been determined. The establishment of the
German Economic Commission as a purely Soviet under-
taking, the currency reform and finally the founding of the
German Democratic Republic on 7 October 1949, marked
the further stages along the path towards a socialist and
democratic people's state. This was finally realised by
means of the total nationalisation and collectivisation of
the means of production, the comprehensive planning of
all economic requirements and the political, military and
economic integration of the new state in the system of
alliances controlled by the Soviet Union.

The DDR became the outpost of the socialist world
against the capitalist system of the West. It was opposed by
the BRD, which was also integrated within a hostile
alliance. This other part of Germany was equally a puppet
of a world power, a political cover for a programme of
massive rearmament, and was held together as a political
and state organisation by an ideological consciousness of
being in the front line. The BRD, however, was the happy
and complacent recipient of international relief efforts,
and was characterised by a high standard of living and
restorative policies implemented and founded in the

127

The Divided Economy: the Fruits of Defeat

spirit of the 'Christian and Western tradition of freedom'.

The BRD and the DDR, and therefore the division of Germany, were a result of the politics of occupation and evidence of the fact that, although the Allies had indeed won the war, they had lost the peace.

In the Western zones there was no move towards land reform. Right from the start there had been a renunciation of radical measures, and although a start had been made in dismantling industrial plant, particularly in the French zone, individual firms in the first instance were able to continue production without hindrance. In addition, the German representatives on the mixed dismantling commissions had the opportunity, particularly in the British zone, of revising the list of concerns to be dismantled in many major areas. By the time the policy was to have been finally implemented in the Western zones, there had been in the intervening period a change in political opinion in America. Now it was no longer Germany that was viewed as enemy number one, but Russia, which had systematically extended its influence over Eastern Europe. It had thereby provoked a revision of American policy towards Europe and Germany. But even before this policy change, the economic and social development of the Western zones had already been directed along different paths.

Practically all those West German concerns which had been initially confiscated were able to restart production soon after the capitulation, and the material assets created by the re-activation of the production process were partly allotted to the Germans as export credits. The concerns were also unaffected by expropriation. The victors, in line with their capitalist system, were content with administrative trustee agencies, on which – alongside the representatives of the work force who demanded a nationalisation of the economy and a comprehensive reduction in the powers of the 'big capitalist and noble families of the Ruhr' – there sat members of these very same families: Springorum, Hoesch, Jucho etc. As a result, the thread of continuity was never broken in the West. The trade

128

unions, political parties and employer associations were restored and policies were initially initiated in those areas where the democratic tradition seemed to have been preserved in a world which effectively represented Christian-social, liberal-democratic and socialist trade-union principles.

Corresponding to the reform of the political order, which was now organised along democratic lines according to the intentions of the occupying powers, the re-organisation of the economy was similarly not pushed through with the degree of radicalism that had originally been planned. The nationalisation of the key industries, the abolition of syndicates, the breakup of corporate cartels, and the implementation of the workers' right to co-determination never progressed more than half-way, just as in the case of the dismantling policy. Although the process of dispersal was initiated, with the majority of cartels dispersed by 1947/8, and although in Hessen and the North Rhine province nationalisation laws were actually passed, the legislation was never in fact applied. Shortly afterwards the coal, iron and steel concerns, the electrical firms and the large banking houses joined together again 'in their old glory and under their old names' (K. Borchardt). What in fact remained of the process of deconcentration was the proliferation of associations which were economically ineffective and which were able to operate on a more profitable basis by means of cartel agreements.

The causative reasons for this development are not only to be found in the intensified tension between East and West. Without doubt this tension was one factor influencing the Western allies in their decision to put a stop to the hard policies of retribution and to initiate a form of co-operative action with 'their' Germans. This involved co-operation with the de-nazified entrepreneurs who had remained in leading positions and with the workers who wanted to see nationalisation and 'decartelisation' of concerns postponed until a later date, because they believed that production could be more quickly revived on the basis of the old economic system than if experiments had first to be made within the context of a new socialist economy.

The Divided Economy: the Fruits of Defeat

But of no less importance in this context was the threat of a severe economic crisis in the American economy, which could only be avoided – in the opinion of Washington and New York – if Europe were cured economically, and indeed as quickly as possible. Only with Germany integrated within the world economic system, and with a trading partner who was both politically stable and financially solvent, would it be possible to create a catalyst which would fuse the European nations together in opposition to Soviet aspirations, as well as opening up an important market area for the American economy. The enemy of yesterday had to become the ally of today, just as the ally of yesterday had now become today's enemy.

The European Recovery Program was the product of such considerations. The funds from the Marshall Plan began to flow towards Europe. The Western Europeans had the opportunity of borrowing money to finance imports of the most essential goods from the USA, and the Americans were able to create for themselves a market area in Western Europe and establish a firm foothold. A prerequisite for the effectiveness of this American counter-plan to Stalin's concept of Europe was the rapid stabilisation of economic and monetary relations in the Western zones, where the problem of the refugees and the shortage of housing continued to dominate as before. 'The German', it was said, 'does not hope, he hungers and freezes'. The secret kings of this period of extreme distress were the peasants, and a system of barter and a black market had come to replace the exchange of goods and cash. Germany itself, after the ruins had been cleared away, was a tidied-up desert. The boon of American dollars now poured over this desert. The 'management of scarcity' and the 'dammed-up inflation' were now effectively curtailed by a new cut in the currency, which signified the start of an economic boom in the Western zones which had not been anticipated. This step, however, destroyed the last thread of unity – which had been in any case questionable – within the economic structure of the four zones: namely, the existence of a uniform currency.

The division of the former Empire in the economic

130

sphere, as laid out in the economic structure of the various zones and the interzonal system of administration, was thereby completed. Whereas the Eastern part was forced to bear the costs of the war right until the bitter end and sought to build up its new social and economic order under conditions of extrene destitution, coercion, insecurity and widespread sacrifice, the West, characterised by an immense backlog of demand and supported by the advantages of an enforced modernisation of its industrial plant, was able to extend its productive output and to raise its level of exports. It was also able to forcibly implement a stable currency policy, to link itself to federalist traditions which were only partly of a democratic and parliamentary nature, and to find a state organisation which could be easily integrated in the system of political economic and military alliances led by the USA.

In the course of this doubtlessly magnificent process of consolidation and economic growth which became synonymous with political stabilisation, the traditional order was restored in the West. In the East, by way of contrast, something completely new arose under Soviet control. In the West, despite numerous initial attempts at nationalisation, a close continuity was preserved in the economic and social order. The social market economy emerged as the remnant of the 'revolutionary synthesis', of 'those organically developed elements of the market economy which had been preserved' and the 'system of economic planning and control' (L. Erhard). America's assistance precluded not only a new organisation and restructuring of the German economic and social order, but also prevented any simple changes. Despite, or perhaps more correctly because of, the highly-praised economic miracle, the opportunities of a shift in emphasis to new industries were lost during the 1950s, particularly in the field of power supply.

As in the sphere of foreign policy, the young state trusted its American ally in the economic field and saw its future secured in a policy based on military strength and traditional industries, such as coal. The unconditional acceptance of its partisan membership of the Western

131

camp, the unconditional investment of its long-term credit in the extension of the large-scale concerns in the coal-mining industry, in metallurgy, the traditional sources of energy and car construction, effectively helped to lay the seeds of the 1960s crisis in the Ruhr region.

Indeed, it is true that with the end of the war, with the absolute defeat of Germany and the division of Europe, the great dilemma of the German economy which stemmed from the nineteenth century had finally been resolved. The primary sector in Germany could no longer become the basis for a conservative revival. But it now became apparent that those sections of the coal, iron and steel and other industries, which had emerged in the nineteenth century in the forefront of the technical revolution, had now themselves become a force resisting further technical development in the face of an increasing industrial exploitation of atomic power, new principles of distribution, and increased demand for education and a higher level of skilled technical knowledge. The new structural crisis to which this gave rise made it quite clear that, in the case of the BRD twenty years after the end of the war, the political and economic system imported by the victorious powers – at least in their restorative form as implemented in Germany – constituted far more of a hindrance than a stimulant to secure economic and social development. Today the danger exists once again that an economic crisis could become a crisis of the state, where only the all-embracing powers of the state could be expected to provide a possible solution.

Appendix:
Some Important Biographies

P. C. W. Beuth (1781–1853)
Commonly regarded as the 'father of Prussian industry', his initial training was derived largely as a principal assistant to Kunth and Maassen in the period 1814–18. The extensive travels which he undertook in the United Kingdom during this period are typical of an important means by which technical developments initiated in England during the Industrial Revolution were quickly transferred to Continental countries. As head of the Department of Trade and Industry, he was to play a crucial role in the promotion of the machine age in Prussia. His overall influence was heightened by his involvement in three other important institutions – the Technical Commission, the Berlin Technical Institute and the Association for the Promotion of Industrial Knowledge in Prussia.

Stephan Born (1824–98)
Born was an important supporter of Marx and Engels. After a period as an apprentice book printer, he took over the leadership of the 'Arbeiterverein' after the outbreak of the revolution in Berlin in 1848. On 23 August 1848 he called for the establishment of a general congress of German workers, which did in fact meet in September 1848.

This body in turn founded the first political organisation of the working class in Germany in the form of the 'Allgemeine deutsche Arbeiter-Verbrüderung', which soon had 170 local affiliated organisations and a central control committee in Leipzig where Born was its president. However, the organisation moved rapidly away from the original Marxist tenets, coming to favour social reform within the context of a democratically organised state. (cf. S. Born, *Errinerungen eines Achtundvierzigers*, Leipzig: 1898.)

A. Borsig (1804–54)

After an initial training in Egell's works, he set up his own concern in the form of a small machine-building works in Berlin in 1837. Although his early reputation stemmed from the installation of pump machinery for the fountains in the palace of Sans Souci, his main contribution lay in the sphere of locomotive construction. The first machine built was constructed in 1842 and at the time of his death the works had turned out over 500 locomotives. In 1850 he also purchased the Moabit engineering works and in addition the Seehandlung's shipbuilding yard. See W. O. Henderson, *The State and the Industrial Revolution in Prussia, 1740–1870*, Liverpool: 1967. p. 114.

R. W. von Bunsen (1811–99)

Bunsen succeeded to the new Chair in the Philosophical Faculty at Heidelberg, after the Chair of Chemistry previously held by Leopold Gmelin in the Medical Faculty had been discontinued. He had previously taught at Marburg, where his students had included Hermann Kolbe, F. A. Genth, Frankland and John Tyndall. By 1855 the number of students had risen from an initial 20 to 60, and by the early 1860s this figure had in turn been surpassed, when 66 students were enrolled. The single course of lectures, dealing with general experimental chemistry, provided a complete survey of the field of inorganic chemistry. Bunsen was ennobled for his services to chemistry, and in particular his contribution to spectrum analysis.

F. A. J. Egells (1788–1854)

After an extensive tour of England (in 1820), he established with a Prussian financial subsidy an iron foundry and engineering works in the Lindenstrasse in Berlin. Although constrained by the expansion of the firm to move the premises at a later date, he constructed a hydraulic press in 1824 and produced his first steam engine in 1825. The concern was particularly important in the sphere of engineering, not simply because of its own products, but also for the training it provided to a long list of other individuals, such as Borsig and Wohlert, who were further to extend the scope of engineering as a whole in Germany.

G. Egestorff (1802–68)

Egestorff was one of the major large-scale industrialists in the first half of the nineteenth century. Initially with interests in tile and brick manufacture and coal mining, he diversified into the timber trade and sugar refining, with the purchase of a sugar refinery in Bremen. He was also instrumental in the improvement of water transport on the Leine, Aller and Weser. Equally after 1846, the concern was a substantial supplier of locomotives. By 1867 the firm had manufactured 324 locomotives and over 650 steam engines and steam pumps. Further diversification had been realised in 1839 with the acquisition of a chemical factory. Egestorff was also typical of his class in a philanthropical capacity, setting up special kitchens for feeding the impoverished members of the working class.

F. Harkort (1793–1880)

As an individual entrepreneur, Harkort was an outstanding figure of the early nineteenth century, involved in a number of areas of important development. He provided the engines for the river steamships which were put into service on the River Weser in 1836. Slightly earlier, in 1829, he had advocated the construction of a railway from Rheine to Lippstadt and was involved in the same year with plans for a proposed route from Düsseldorf to Elberfeld. He was instrumental in the introduction of the puddling process into Westphalia (at Watter in 1826) and contributed significantly to the development of a machine-building industry in Germany.

August von Hofmann (1818–92)

In 1845 Hofmann was appointed professor at the Royal College of Chemistry (London), having started investigations into coal-tar in Giessen, which he later continued in London. He stayed in London for 20 years, his most fruitful years being between 1845 and 1852, when he published numerous papers, sometimes in collaboration with some of his students such as Georg Merck, F. A. Abel, Warren de la Rue and E. C. Nicholson. Another student, W. H. Perkin (1833–1907) attempted a synthetic preparation of quinine, working from an earlier suggestion by Hofmann, which led directly to the development of aniline purple. During the peak of his productive work, Hofmann had 40 students in his London laboratory. When he left for Berlin in 1865 he had effectively accomplished the transplanting of the Giessen tradition in London, and it could justifiably be claimed that he had laid the foundations for a new system of chemical education in London. He was also ennobled for his general services in the promotion of chemistry.

F. A. Kekule (1829–96)

Organic chemistry was not taught at Bunsen's institute. Those students wishing to study this branch of chemistry by and large attended the classes of the junior staff members, particularly those of Kekule in the period 1856–8. By the 1860s, however, Kekule was teaching about 60 students in his laboratory at Bonn. He was particularly important shedding light on the theory of coal-tar chemistry, by propounding the theory of a hexagonally shaped benzene molecule with alternate double bonds (1865). This had been hailed as one of the fundamental discoveries in chemistry, and the idea was taken up by Bayer during his investigations into the indigo problem in the 1880s. During the 1850s and 1860s, Kekule was an important contributor to the 'Annalen der Chemie'. He was also ennobled for his services to chemistry.

W. E. von Ketteler (1811–77)
As Bishop of Mainz (after 1850) he was instrumental in bringing people's attention to the 'social question' as the most important contemporary issue. The solution to this problem, however, lay not in social reform and state legislation, but in a greater profusion of 'love' and the conquering of 'unbelief'. He supported in general Lassalle's concept of how the working class movement should develop. By the 1860s Ketteler had also become a strong opponent of liberalism, but he was nevertheless instrumental in providing Catholics with the necessary impetus to reassess the social question with greater understanding.

G. R. Kirchoff (1824–87)
Kirchoff provided an important contribution to the development of spectrum analysis. His work was primarily concerned with the problems of emission, absorption and heat dispersal. At the same time his published lectures on mathematical physics, re-published in a second edition in Leipzig in 1877, had an important influence on scientific circles in Germany.

Adolf Kolping (1813–65)
Having started as an apprentice cobbler, Kolping became a priest in 1845, and became important in the Catholic 'Handwerkgesellenverein' (the Association of Handicraft Apprentices) which had been founded in the autumn of 1846. By 1851 the original organisation had been transformed into the 'Katholischer Gesellenverein' (the Catholic Association of Apprentices), which by 1855 had 104 local groups with a total membership of about 12,000. The general emphasis was on the importance of religious instruction, professional advancement and social contacts. Kolping's claim to fame lies not in his theoretical analysis of contemporary problems, but in his practical social work.

Appendix: Some Important Biographies

J. G. Koppe (1782–1863)

Koppe was important in his overall coverage of the field of agricultural science, particularly in his major published work, *Unterricht im Ackerbau und in der Viehzucht*, which appeared in three parts in 1841/2. Two volumes were specifically devoted to arable and livestock farming. He was especially noted for his active participation in the discovery of the practicability of different farming systems and his contribution to the development of the doctrine of valuation.

Alfr(i)ed Krupp (1812–87)

Having inherited a small iron works in Essen, successive generations of the family were to develop the enterprise into one of the most significant industrial complexes in the whole of Germany. Although the initial profits for the running of the firm came significantly from trade, the Krupp concern was at first important in the introduction of the production of cast steel. The number of monographs dealing with the Krupp concern are comparatively legion, including W. Berdrow, *Alfred Krupp*, English translation: 1930; and B. Engelmann, *Krupp. Legenden und Wirklichkeit*, Munich: 1970.

G. J. C. Kunth (1757–1829)

As General Commissioner for Commerce in Prussia, having entered the Prussian civil service in 1789, Kunth was to have a major role in the restructuring of trade and commerce in the early nineteenth century. He advocated the founding of a number of trade schools and succeeded in establishing a royal commercial college in Berlin. The technical school at Magdeburg was largely a result of Kunth's activities. His memorandum of March 1817 played a significant part in the abolition of internal dues in Prussia incorporated in Maassen's tariff law of 1818. He was also involved in plans for a new Technical Commission in 1808 and in the formation of the Association for the promotion of Industrial Knowledge in Prussia. Cf. F. G. P. Goldschmidt, *Das Leben des Staatsraths Kunth*, Berlin: 1881.; W. O Henderson, *The State and the Indus-*

Appendix: Some Important Biographies

trial Revolution in Prussia, 1740–1870, Liverpool: 1967
pp. 97–9.

Justus von Liebig (1803–73)
Having studied at Bonn, Erlangen and Paris (in the laboratory of Gay-Lussac), he went on to found the Giessen
school in Germany, with its emphasis on experimental
chemistry. His reputation was effectively founded on two
major publications of 1840, and although his work was
initially ignored by the Prussian government, Austria sent
individual students to Giessen for training. His contribution to the development of organic chemistry was
vital, particularly in the discovery of choloroform and
chlorine.

J. Mayer
Mayer was one of the major producers of cast steel in the
Ruhr in the 1840s (in company with Alfred Krupp and
Jacobi). His works at Bochum also specialised to some
degree in the production of cast church bells.

F. Schichau (1814–96)
After the completion of studies in England, Schichau
established an engineering works at Elbing on the Baltic.
His firm gained an important reputation with the installation of machinery for rolling-mills, sawmills and sugar
refineries. He built the first steam-dredger in Germany in
the 1840s and the first screw-propelled steamship to be
launched in Prussia (1855). W. O. Henderson, *op. cit.*, pp.
114–15.

Max Schönleutner (1777–1831)
From 1803 Schönleutner was director of the model farm at
Weihenstephan (Bavaria) and founded an important
school for the training of agriculturalists there. In 1810 he
became the chief administrator of the state farms at
Schleissheim, Weihenstephan and Fürstenried.

J. C. R. v. dem Kleefelde Schubarth (1734–87)
Schubarth was an important forerunner of Thaer. On the

basis of experience from extensive tours of Europe, Schubarth was to play an important role in the general introduction of clover and potatoes into the traditional three-field rotation pattern in Germany and Austria-Hungary. In 1784 he was ennobled by Kaiser Leopold for a prize essay on the cultivation of fodder crops.

M. E. Solvay (1838–1922)

His father owned a small salt refining plant at Rebecq-Rognon in Brabant, and his uncle was the director of a small gasworks at Schaarbeck (outside Brussels). Having joined his uncle's enterprise, Solvay was convinced of the efficiency of the 'wet' method in the production of soda (using brine), and he devised a practical carbonator (known as the Solvay tower) and a still to recover ammonia. An experimental plant was working as early as 1861, although problems connected with the control of the temperature in the process created unexpected difficulties. Operations at Couillet did not really begin until January 1865, but by the early 1870s this ammonia-soda process was considered universally as the best. The plant was copied by Ludwig Mond in 1872 after an agreement on royalties and thus found its way to England.

F. Steinbeis (1807–93)

In charge of the Stumm ironworks at Neunkirchen (from 1842), he was instrumental in introducing the coal-fired blast furnace into Germany. In 1848 he was appointed technical adviser to the Württemberg government in the newly-created 'Centralstelle für Gewerbe und Handel'. From 1860 to 1880 Steinbeis was the managing director of the 'Commission für die gewerblichen Fortbildungsschulen', where his main responsibility, apart from improving the level and extent of technical and industrial training, was to contribute to increased production in Württemberg and to secure a wider market for Württemberg's products.

A. Thaer (1752–1828)

Often known as the father of scientific agriculture in Germany, Thaer derived much of his initial information from the English agronomes, and in particular from Young. His basic ideas are to be found in his most famous publication, *Die Grundsätze der rationellen Landwirtschaft*, and he built up a teaching system largely founded on the basis of British discoveries. With his emphasis on the farm as a unit of business, with a given availability of the factors of production, his writings played a major role in the increasing commercialisation of the primary sector in Germany. (Cf. J. Nou, *The Development of Agricultural Economics in Europe*, Uppsala: 1967, *passim*.)

J. H. von Thünen (1783–1850)

He was one of the classical names in agricultural economics. Although his work was relatively neglected by contemporaries, his mode of investigating the functioning of the agricultural system contained many ideas the significance of which were only to be realised later. His theory of price formation and his treatment of the mechanism of price adjustment are particularly outstanding.

Wilhelm Weitling (1808–71)

Weitling was one of the foremost of German socialists in the period prior to 1848. His writings betray the influence of Saint-Simon, Fourier and Owen. Having served as an apprentice tailor, he effectively determined the political orientation of the 'Bund der Gerechten' in Paris (later known as the 'Bund der Kommunisten'). In a major publication of 1842, he envisaged the necessity of a dictatorship to cope effectively with the problems generated by the transition period from revolution to communism. In 1843, he voiced the future possibility of a communist society dependent on the exchange of goods. His general emphasis lay on the importance of equality and the abolition of money and national frontiers, but at times there were still traces of his own craft origins in his defence of handicraft producers and small shopkeepers. His overall influence tended to disappear after 1843, and in 1846 he emigrated to America, after an argument with Marx and Engels. Although he temporarily returned in 1848, he finally returned to America and withdrew from the political arena completely.

J. H. Wichern (1801–81)

Wichern was essentially a conservative evangelical. He attempted the regeneration of contemporary society by means of an association of religious and charitable Christians, with an emphasis on the traditional custom of private charitable gifts to the poor and destitute. During the mid 1840s, however, these ideas were commonly followed by most state officials in Prussia and other German states.

G. G Winkler (1820–77)

As professor of minerology at the Industrial School in Munich, Winkler was primarily concerned with the development of the science of mining in general, and particularly in Iceland and the Alps.

Bibliography

Compiled by W. R. Lee

The following bibliography is designed to provide a comprehensive list of publications in English on the subject of German economic history during the period covered by the text. It is designed to dispel the myth that a study of Germany economic history is made difficult by the absence of sufficient secondary material. At the same time this has entailed a substantial restructuring of the original bibliography. Section I contains works by authors cited in the text. Section 2 contains relevant works written in the English language and compiled specifically for the purpose of this English edition of Böhme's work.

Section 1

Abel, W., Geschichte der deutschen Landwirtschaft vom
    frühen Mittelalter bis zum 19. Jahrhundert. Stuttgart:
    1962.
—— Agrarkrisen und Agrarkonjunkturen. Second edition,
    Hamburg-Stuttgart: 1966.
Borchardt, K., 'Zur Frage des Kapitalmangels in der ersten
    Hälfte des 19. Jahrhunderts in Deutschland', in
    Jahrbücher für Nationalökonomie und Statistik, Bd. 173.
Born, K. E. (Ed.), Moderne deutsche Wirtschaftsgeschichte.
    Köln-Berlin: 1967.
—— 'Der soziale und wirtschaftliche Strukturwandel
    Deutschlands am Ende des 19. Jahrhunderts', in

Bibliography

*Vierteljahrschrift für Sozial-und Wirtschaftsgeschichte,
50.* Wiesbaden: 1963 (VSWG).
—— *Staat und Sozialpolitik seit Bismarcks Sturz.* Wiesbaden:
1957.
—— *Die deutsche Bankenkrise 1931, Finanzen und Politik.*
München: 1967.
Conze, W., 'Die Wirkungen der liberalen Agrarreformen auf
die Volksordnung in Mitteleuropa im 19. Jahrhundert',
in *Vierteljahrschrift für Sozial-und Wirtschaftsge-
schichte, 38.* 1951.
—— 'Vom "Pöbel" zum "Proletariat",' *Sozialgeschichtliche
Voraussetzungen für den Sozialismus in Deutschland.*
VSWG, 41: 1954.
—— *Die Strukturgeschichte des technisch-industriellen
Zeitalters.* Köln: 1957.
—— (Ed.), *Staat und Gesellschaft im deutschen Vormärz
1815–1848.* Stuttgart: 1962.
—— 'Nation und Gesellschaft. Zwei Grundbegriffe der
revolutionären Epoche', in *Historische Zeitschrift, 198:*
1964 (HZ).
Dahrendorf, R., *Soziale Klassen und Klassenkonflikt in der
industriellen Gesellschaft.* Stuttgart: 1957.
Fischer, F., *Griff nach der Weltmacht. Die Kriegszielpolitik
des kaiserlichen Deutschlands 1914/18.* Düsseldorf: 1961.
Fischer, W., *Der Staat und die Anfänge der
Industrialisierung in Baden 1800–1850.* Vol. 1, Berlin:
1962.
—— 'Soziale Unterschichten im Zeitalter der
Frühindustrialisierung', in *International Review of
Social History*, VII: 1963.
Hintze, O., *Gesammelte Abhandlungen.* Ed. by G. Oestreich,
Göttingen: 1962–5.
Jantke, C., *Der vierte Stand. Die gestaltenden Kräfte der
deutschen Arbeiterbewegung im 19. Jahrhundert.*
Freiburg: 1955.
—— /Hilger, D. *Die Eigentumslosen. Der deutsche
Pauperismus und die Emanzipationskrise in Darstellung
und Deutung der zeitgenössischen Literatur.* Freiburg:
1965.
Kehr, E., *Der Primat der Innenpolitik.* Ed. by H-U. Wehler,
Berlin: 1965.
Kellenbenz, H., 'Von den Wirtschaftsstufentheorie zu den
Wachstumsstadien Rostows', in *Zeitschrift für die
gesamte Staatswissenschaft*, Bd. 120. Tübingen: 1964.

144

Kosellek, R., *Kritik und Krise, ein Beitrag zur Pathogenese der bürgerlichen Welt.* Freiburg/München: 1959.
—— *Preussen zwischen Reform und Revolution 1786–1848.* Stuttgart: 1967.
Kotowski, G., *Friedrich Ebert. Eine politische Biographie.* Bd. I., Wiesbaden: 1963.
Kroll, G., *Von der Weltwirtschaftskrise zur Staatskonjunktur.* Berlin: 1958.
Landes, D. S., 'Technological change and development in Western Europe, 1750–1914', in *The Cambridge Economic History of Europe*, Bd. 6, 11.
—— 'Entrepreneurship in Advanced Industrial Countries: the Anglo-German Rivalry', in *Entrepreneurship and Economic Growth.* Harvard: 1954.
Lütge, F., *Deutsche Sozial-und Wirtschaftsgeschichte. Ein Ueberblick.* Berlin-Heidelberg-New York: 1966.
—— (Ed.), *Die wirtschaftliche Situation in Deutschland und Oesterreich um die Wende vom 18. zum 19. Jahrhundert.* Stuttgart: 1964.
Ritter, G. A., 'Die Arbeiterbewegung im Wilhelminischen Reich. Die Sozial-demokratische Partei und die freien Gewerkschaften, 1890–1900', in *Studien zur Europäischen Geschichte am Friedrich-Meinecke-Institut der FU Berlin.* Berlin: 1959.
Rostow, W. W. *Stadien wirtschaftlichen Wachstums. Eine Alternative zur marxistischen Entwicklungstheorie.* Göttingen: 1960.
—— *The Process of Economic Growth.* New York: 1952.
—— (Ed.), *The Economics of Take-off into Sustained Growth.* New York: 1964.
Rosenberg, A., *Entstehung der Weimarer Republik.* Frankfurt/M: 1961.
—— *Geschichte der Weimarer Republik.* Frankfurt/M: 1961.
Rosenberg, H., 'Die Weltwirtschaftskrisis von 1857–1859, Stuttgart, 1934.
—— Grosse Depression und Bismarckzeit', in *Wirtschaftsablauf, Gesellschaft und Politik in Mitteleuropa.* Berlin: 1967.
—— 'Die "Demokratisierung" der Rittergutsbesitzerklasse', in *Festgabe für H. Herzfeld.* Berlin: 1958.
Schumpter, J., *Business Cycles. A Theoretical, Historical and Statistical Analysis of the Capitalist Process.* 2 vols., New York: 1939.

Bibliography

Stadelmann, R., *Deutschland und Westeuropa*. Laupheim: 1948.

—— /Fischer, W., 'Die Bildungswelt des deutschen Handwerkers um 1800', in *Studien zur Soziologie des Kleinbürgers im Zeitalter Goethes*. Berlin: 1955.

—— *Soziale und politische Geschichte der Revolution von 1848*. München: 1948.

Stolper, G./Häuser, K./Borchardt, K., *Deutsche Wirtschaft seit 1870*. Tübingen: 1964.

Treue, W., 'Wirtschafts-und Sozialgeschichte Deutschlands im 19. Jahrhundert', in Gebhardt, B., *Handbuch der Deutschen Geschichte*, Bd. 3: 1960.

—— *Die Geschichte der Ilseder Hütte*. Peine: 1960.

—— *Wirtschaftsgeschichte der Neuzeit. Im Zeitalter der industriellen Revolution 1700–1960*. Stuttgart: 1962.

—— 'Wirtschaftszustände und Wirtschaftspolitik in Preussen 1815–1825'. VSWG, Beiheft 31: 1937.

—— *Deutsche Wirtschaft und Politik 1933–1945*. Hannover-Braunschweig: 1963.

Wagemann, E., *Economic Rhythm. A Theory of Business Cycles*. New York: 1930.

Weinstock, U., *Das Problem der Kondratieff-Zyklen. Ein Beitrag zur Entwicklung einer Theorie der langen Wellen und ihre Bedeutung*. Berlin-München: 1964.

Zorn, W., 'Wirtschafts-und sozialgeschichtliche Zusammenhänge der deutschen Reichsgründungszeit 1850–1879'. HZ, 197: 1963.

—— 'Typen und Entwicklungskräfte des deutschen Unternehmertums im 19. Jahrhundert', in VSWG, 44: 1957.

Section 2
Journal abbreviations:

HZ	Historische Zeitschrift
VSWG	Vierteljahrschrift für Sozial-und Wirtschaftsgeschichte
WA	Weltwirtschaftliches Archiv
AHR	Agricultural History Review
BHR	Business History Review
CEH	Central European History
EHR	Economic History Review
EEH	Explorations in Entrepreneurial History
HJ	Historical Journal
JCH	Journal of Contemporary History

Bibliography

ILR   International Labor Review
JEH   Journal of Economic History
JEEH   Journal of European Economic History
JIH   Journal of Interdisciplinary History
JMH   Journal of Modern History
K   Kyklos
PS   Population Studies
QJE   Quarterly Journal of Economics

Adelmann, G., 'Structural changes in the Rhenish linen and
    cotton trades at the outset of Industrialization', in *Essays
    in European Economic History (EEEH)*. Edited by
    Crouzet, F., Chaloner, W. H., and Stern, W. M., London:
    1969.
Allen, W. S., *The Nazi Seizure of Power. The experience of a
    single German town 1930—35*. Chicago: 1965.
Anderson, E. N., *The social and political conflict in Prussia,
    1858/64*. Lincoln: 1954.
Andie, S., *The Growth of Government Expenditure in
    Germany since the Unification*. Finanzarchiv: 1964.
Angel-Volkov, S., 'The "Decline of the German Handicrafts"
    – another reappraisal.' VSWG: 1974.
Armytage, W. H. G., 'Some aspects of technical training and
    social improvement in Germany from 1815 to 1914', in
    Vocational Aspects: 1960.
Arndt, H. W., *The economic lessons of the 1930s*. London:
    1963 (1944).
Ashley, W. J., *The Progress of the German Working Classes
    in the last quarter of a century*: 1904.

Balogh, T., 'The National Economy of Germany', in *Economic
    Journal*: 1938.
Barkin, K. D., *The Controversy over German Industrialization
    1890–1902*. Chicago: 1970.
Barret-Whale, P., *Joint Stock Banks in Germany*. London: 1930.
Baxter, A. L. Y., 'Some economic aspects of rearmament', in
    International Labour Review: 1938.
Beer, J. J., *The Emergence of the German Dye Industry*.
    Illinois: 1959.
Block, H., 'German methods of allocating Raw Materials', in
    Social Research: 1942.
—— 'Man-power allocation in Germany', in *Harvard Business
    Review*: 1943.
Böhme, H., 'Big Business, Pressure groups and Bismarck's

Bibliography

turn to Protectionism, 1873–1879', in *Historical Journal*.
X: 1967.
Bowen, R. H., 'The Role of Government and Private
Enterprise in German Industrial Growth', in *Journal of
Economic History (JEH)*. Supplement: 1950.
—— *German theories of the Corporative State, with special
reference to the period 1870—1919*. New York: 1947.
Brady, A., *The rationalisation movement in German
industry, a study in the evolution of economic planning*.
Berkeley: 1953.
Brady, R. A., 'Policies of Manufacturing Spitzenverbände', in
Political Science Quarterly: 1941.
—— 'The economic impact of Imperial Germany's industrial
policy', in *JEH*. Supplement: 1943.
Brinkmann, C., 'The Place of Germany in the economic
History of the 19th century', in *Economic History Review
(EHR)*: 1933.
Bruck, W. F., *Social and Economic History of Germany from
William II to Hitler, 1888—1938*. Cardiff: 1938.
Bry, G., *Wages in Germany, 1871–1945*. Princeton: 1960.

Cameron, R. E., 'Founding the Bank of Darmstadt', in
Explorations in Entrepreneurial History (EEH): 1956.
Carroll, B. A., 'Germany disarmed and re-arming, 1935–1935'
in *Journal of Peace Research*: 1966.
—— *Design for Total War. Arms and economics in the Third
Reich*. Moaten: 1968.
Cecil, L., *Albert Ballin: Business and Politics in Imperial
Germany, 1888–1918*. Princeton: 1967.
Child, F. C., *The Theory and Practice of Exchange Control in
Germany*. The Hague: 1958.
Clapham, J. H., *The Economic Development of France and
Germany, 1815–1914*. Fourth ed., Cambridge: 1955.
Cole, T., 'The Evolution of the German Labor Front', in
Political Science Quarterly: 1937.
Colm, G., 'Why the Papen plan for Economic Recovery
failed', in *Social Research*: 1934.
Conze, W., 'The effects of nineteenth century Liberal agrarian
reforms on social structure in Central Europe', in *EEEH*.

Dawson, W. H., *Bismarck and State Socialism: an exposition
of the social and economic legislation in Germany since
1870*. London: 1891.
—— *Protection in Germany*. London: 1904.

—— The German Workman. London: 1906.

Dehn, R. M. R., The German Cotton Industry. Manchester: 1913.

Bernburg, H. J., 'Some basic aspects of the German debt settlement', in Journal of Finance: 1953.

Desai, A. V., Real Wages in Germany, 1871–1913. Oxford: 1968.

Dessauer, M., 'The German Bank Act of 1934', Review of Economic Studies: 1935.

Dorman, J. R., 'Hitler's economic mobilisation', in Military Review: 1953/4.

Dorn, W. L., 'The Prussian Bureaucracy in the 18th century', in Political Science Quarterly: 1931/2.

Ebenstein, W., 'Employment of women in Germany under the Nationalist Socialist Regime', in International Labor Review: 1944.

Ellis, H., 'Exchange control in Germany', in Quarterly Journal of Economics (QJE). Supplement: 1940.

—— Exchange Control in Central Europe. Cambridge: 1941.

Eucken, W., 'On the theory of the centrally administered Economy: an analysis of the German experiments, in Economica: 1948.

Falkus, M. E., 'The German Business Cycle in the 1920s', in EHR: 1975.

Feldman, G. D., Army, Industry and Labor In Germany, 1914–1918. Princeton: 1966.

Fischer, W., 'Social Tensions at early stages of Industrialization,' in Comparative studies in Social History: 1966.

—— 'Government activity and industrialisation in Germany (1815–1870)', in W. W. Rostow (Ed.), The Economics of take-off into sustained growth. London: 1971 (reprint).

—— 'The German Zollverein, a case study of a customs union, in Kyklos (K): 1960.

Flink, S., The German Reichsbank and Economic Germany. New York: 1930.

Ford, G. F., Stein and the Era of Reform in Prussia: 1922.

Gagliardo, J. G., From Pariah to Patriot: the Changing Image of the German Peasant, 1770–1840. Lexington: 1969.

Gellately, R., The Politics of Economic Despair. Shopkeepers and German Politics, 1890–1914. London: 1974.

Bibliography

Gerschenkron, A., *Bread and Democracy in Germany*. New York: 1965 (reprint).

Giordani, P., *The German Colonial Empire: its beginning and ending*. London: 1916.

Goebel, O. H., *German Raw Material Economy in the World War*. New Haven: 1930.

Grebler, L., 'Work Creation Policy in Germany, 1932–35', in *International Labor Review (ILR)*: 1937.

Grunberg, E., 'The mobilization of capacity and resources of small-scale enterprises in Germany', *Journal of Business*: 1941.

Grunberger, R., *A Social History of the Third Reich*. London: 1971.

Gurland, A. R. L., 'Technological trends and economic structure under National Socialism', in *Studies in Philosophy and Social Science*: 1941.

Haber, L. F., *The Chemical Industry during the nineteenth century*. Oxford: 1958.

Hackett, A., 'The German Women's Movement and Suffrage, 1890–1914: a study of National Feminism', in R. J. Bezucha (Ed.), *Modern European Social History (MESH)*. Lexington: 1972.

Hallgarten, G. W. F., 'Adolf Hitler and the German Heavy Industry, 1931–33', in *Journal of Economic History (JEH)*: 1952.

Haines, G., 'German influence upon scientific Instruction in England 1867–1887', in *Victorian Studies*: 1958.

Hamburger, L., *How Nazi Germany has Mobilised and Controlled Labor*. Washington: 1940.

Hamerow, T. S., *Restoration, Revolution, Reaction*. Princeton: 1958 (1967).

—— *The Social Foundations of German Unification*. 2 vols., Princeton: 1969/72.

Hammen, O. J., 'Economic and social factors in the Prussian Rhineland in 1848', in *American Historical Review*: 1949.

Hardach, K. W., 'Some remarks on German economic historiography', in *Journal of European Economic History (JEEH)*: 1972.

Harriss, C. R. S., *Germany's Foreign Indebtedness*. London: 1935.

Hartmann, H., *Authority and Organisation in German Management*. Princeton: 1959.

Hartsough, M. L. 'The rise and fall of the Stinnes combine', in *Journal of Economic and Business History*: 1931.

Helfferich, K., *Germany's Economic Progress and National Wealth, 1888–1913.* New York: 1914.

Henderson, W. O., 'The Rise of German Industry', in *EHR*: 1935.

—— 'Germany's Trade with her Colonies', in *EHR*: 1938.

—— *Britain and Industrial Europe, 1750–1870: Studies in British Influence on the Industrial Revolution in Western Europe.* Liverpool: 1954.

—— 'The Genesis of the Industrial Revolution in France and Germany in the eighteenth century', in *K*: 1956.

—— 'A nineteenth century approach to a West European Common Market', in *K*: 1957.

—— *The State and the Industrial Revolution in Prussia.* Liverpool: 1967.

—— *The Rise of German Industrial Power, 1834–1914.* London: 1975.

Hoffmann, W. G., 'Long-term growth and capital formation in Germany', in F. A. Lutz and D. C. Hague (Eds.), *Theory of Capital*. London: 1961.

—— 'The take-off in Germany', in W. W. Rostow (Ed.), *The Economics of Take-off into Sustained Growth*. London: 1971 (reprint).

Hughes, T., 'Technological Momentum in History: Hydrogenation in Germany, 1898–1933', in *Past and Present*: 1969.

Jacob, H., *German Administration since Bismarck, Central Authority v. Local Autonomy*. New Haven: 1963.

Jagtiani, H. M., *The Role of the State in the Provision of Railways*. London: 1924.

Jankowski, M. D., 'Law, economic policy and private enterprise: the case of the early Ruhr Mining Region, 1766–1865', in *JEEH*: 1973.

Jasny, M. P., 'Some aspects of German agricultural settlement', in *Political Science Quarterly*: 1937.

Jostock, P., 'The long term growth of national income in Germany', in *Income and Wealth. Series V*: 1955.

Keynes, J. M./Ohlin, B., 'Transfer Problems and German Reparations', in *Economic Journal*: 1928.

Kindleberger, C. P., 'German terms of trade by commodity classes and areas', in *Review of Economic Statistics*: 1954.

Bibliography

Kisch, H., 'The textile industries in Silesia and the Rhineland', in *JEH*: 1959.

—— 'The impact of the French Revolution on the Lower Rhine textile districts. Some comments on economic development and social change', in *EHR*: 1963.

—— 'Growth deterrents of a medieval heritage: the Aachen area woollen trade before 1790', *JEH*: 1964.

—— 'Prussian Mercantilism and the rise of the Krefeld silk industry: variations upon an eighteenth century theme', in *Transactions of the American Philosophical Society*: 1968.

—— 'From monopoly to laissez-faire: the early growth of the Wupper Valley textile trade', in *JEEH*: 1972.

Klein, B. H., *Germany's Economic Preparations for War*. Harvard: 1959.

Klein, J. J., 'German money and prices, 1932–44', in M. Friedman (Ed.), *Studies in the Quantity Theory of Money*. Chicago: 1956.

Knauerhase, R., 'The compound steam engine and productivity changes in the German merchant marine fleet, 1871–87', in *JEH*: 1968.

Knodel, J., 'Law, marriage and illegitimacy in nineteenth century Germany', in *Population Studies (PS)*: 1967.

—— Walle, E. v. d., 'Breast feeding, fertility and infant mortality: an analysis of some early German data', in *PS*: 1967.

—— *The Decline of Fertility in Germany, 1871–1939*. Princeton: 1974.

Kocka, J., 'Family and bureaucracy in German industrial management, 1850–1914, Siemens', *Business History Review (BHR)*: 1971.

—— 'The First World War and the "Mittelstand": German artisans and white-collar workers', in *Journal of Contemporary History*: 1973.

Kohn-Bramstedt, E., *Aristocracy and the Middle Class in Germany*. London: 1937.

Kolko, G., 'American Business and Germany, 1930–41', in *Western Political Quarterly*: 1962.

Köllmann, W., 'The population of Germany in the age of industrialism', in H. Moller (Ed.), *Population Movements in Modern European History*. New York: 1964.

—— 'The process of urbanisation in Germany at the height of the industrial period', in *Journal of Contemporary History*: 1969.

Kraehe, E. E., 'Practical politics in the German Confederation: Bismarck and the commerical code', in *Journal of Modern History (JMH)*: 1953.

Kuczynski, J., *Germany: Economic and Labor Conditions under Fascism*. New York: 1941.

Lachmann, K., 'The Hermann Göring Works', in *Social Research*: 1941.

Lambi, I. N., *Free Trade and Protection in Germany, 1868–79*.

Landes, D. S., 'Entrepreneurship in advanced industrial countries: The Anglo-German rivalry', in *Entrepreneurship and Economic Growth*. Cambridge : 1954.

—— 'Industrialisation and economic development in nineteenth century Germany', First International Conference of Economic History, Stockholm: 1960.

Laurie, S., *Private Investment in a Controlled Economy: Germany, 1933–9*. New York: 1947.

Lebovics, H., *Social Conservatism and the Middle Classes in Germany, 1914–33*. Princeton: 1969.

—— ' "Agrarians" versus "Industrializers". Social conservative resistance to Industrialism and Capitalism in late nineteenth century Germany', in *International Review of Social History*: 1967.

Lee, W. R., 'Tax structure and economic growth in Germany (1750–1850)', in *JEEH*: 1975.

—— 'Bastardy and the Socioeconomic Structure of South Germany', in *JIH*: 1977.

Levy, H., *Industrial Germany: a Study of its Monopoly Organisations and their Control by the State*. London: 1935.

Liebel, H., *Enlightened Bureaucracy v. Enlightened Despotism in Baden, 1756–92*. Philadelphia: 1965.

Liefmann, R., *Cartels, Concerns and Trusts*. London: 1932.

Long, D. C., 'Efforts to secure an Austro-German Customs Union in the nineteenth century', in A. B. Boak (Ed.), *University of Michigan Historical Essays*: 1937.

Lotz, W., *The Financial Policy of the German Government during the War*. New Haven: 1927.

Mandelbaum, K., 'An experiment in full employment: controls in the German economy, 1933–8', in *The Economics of Full Employment*. Oxford: 1944.

153

Bibliography

Marburg, T. F., 'Government and business in Germany: public policy towards Cartels', in *BHR*: 1964.

Marquardt, F. D., 'Pauperismus in Germany during the Vormärz', in *Central European History*: 1969.

Maschke, E., 'Outline of the history of German Cartels from 1873 to 1914', in *EEEH*.

Mason, T. W., 'Labour in the Third Reich, 1933–9', in *Past and Present*: 1966.

—— 'The primacy of politics – politics and economics in National Socialist Germany', in S. J. Woolf (Ed.), *The Nature of Fascism*. New York: 1969.

Merlin, S., 'Trends in German economic control since 1933', in *QJE*: 1943.

Milward, A., *The German Economy at War*. London: 1965.

Müller, H.-H., 'Christopher Brown – an English farmer in Brandenburg-Prussia in the eighteenth century', in *Agricultural History Review*: 1969

Muncy, L. W., *The Junker in the Prussian Administration under William II, 1888–1914*. Brown University: 1944.

Musgrave, P. W., *Technical Change, the Labour Force and Education. A Study of the British and German Iron and Steel Industries, 1860–1964*. Oxford: 1967.

Nathan, O., *The Nazi Economic System. Germany's Mobilization for War*, 1943.

—— 'Consumption in Germany during the period of rearmament', in *QJE*: 1942.

Nelson, W. H., *Small Wonder: the amazing story of the Volkswagen*: 1967.

Nettl, J. P., *The Eastern Zone and Soviet Policy in Germany, 1945–50*. London: 1951.

—— 'Economic checks on German Unity', in *Foreign Affairs*: 1952.

Neuburger, H./Stokes, H. H., 'German banks and German growth, 1883–1913: an empirical view', in *JEH*: 1974.

—— 'German banking and Japanese banking: a comparative analysis', in *JEH*: 1975.

Neumann, R. P., 'Industrialisation and sexual behaviour. Some aspects of working class life in Imperial Germany', in *MESH*: 1972.

Northrop, M. B., *Control Policies of the Reichsbank, 1924–33*. New York: 1938 (1968).

Noyes, P. H., *Organisation and Revolution. Working-class*

Associations in the German Revolution of 1848/9.
Princeton: 1966.

Overy, R. J., 'Transportation and rearmament in the Third
Reich', in *Historical Journal*: 1973.
—— 'Cars, roads and economic recovery in Germany, 1932–8',
in *EHR*: 1975.
Orsagh, T. J., 'The probable geographical distribution of
German income, 1882–1963', in *Zeitschrift für die
gesamte Staatswissenschaft*: 1968.

Parker, W. N., 'Entrepreneurial, industrial organisation and
economic growth: a German example', in *JEH*: 1954.
Parsons, T., 'Democracy and social structure in pre-Nazi
Germany', in *Essays in Sociological Theory*. New York:
1954.
Pesmazoglu, J., 'Some international aspects of German
cyclical fluctuations, 1880–1913', in *Weltwirtschaftliches
Archiv (WA)*: 1950.
—— 'A note on the cyclical fluctuations of the volume of
German home investment, 1880–1913', in *Zeitschrift für
die gesamte Staatswissenschaft*: 1951.
Peterson, E. N., *Hjalmar Schacht*. Boston: 1954.
Phelps Brown, E. A./Browne, M. H., *A Century of Pay: the
Course of Pay and Production in France, Germany,
Sweden, United Kingdom and USA, 1860–1960*.
Macmillan: 1968.
Poole, K. E., *German Financial Policies, 1932–39*. Cambridge:
1939.
Pounds, N. J. G., *The Ruhr: a Study in Historical and
Economic Geography*. London: 1952.
—— *The Upper Silesian Industrial Region*. Bloomington: 1958.
Price, A. H., *The Evolution of the Zollverein*. Michigan:
1949.

Ratchford, B. U./Ross, W. D., *Berlin Reparations Assignment*.
Chapel Hill: 1947.
Redlich, F., 'The leaders of the German steam engine
industry during the first hundred years', in *JEH*: 1944.
—— 'An eighteenth century guide for investors', in *Bulletin
of the Business History Society*: 1952.
—— 'A German eighteenth century iron works during its first
100 years', in *Bulletin of the Business History Society*:
1953.

Bibliography

—— 'Entrepreneurship in the initial stages of industrialisation', in *WA*: 1955.

—— 'Academic education for Business: Its development and the contribution of Ignaz Jastrow, 1856–1937', in *BHR*, 1957.

Reichard, R., *Crippled from Birth. German Social Democracy, 1844–1870.* Iowa: 1969.

Reisser, J., *The German Great Banks and their Concentration in Connection with the Economic Development of Germany.* Third Ed., Washington: 1911.

Ringer, F. K., 'Higher education in Germany in the nineteenth century', in *Journal of Contemporary History*: 1967.

Roberts, S. H., *The House that Hitler Built.* London, tenth edition, 1939.

Robertson, W., 'The problem of adjustment in West Germany's balance of payments', in *Quarterly Review of Banca Nazionale del Lavorno*: 1957.

Röhl, J. C. G., 'Higher civil servants in Germany, 1890–1900', in *Journal of Contemporary History*: 1967.

—— *Germany without Bismarck.* Berkeley: 1967.

Rohr, D. G., *The Origins of Social Liberalism in Germany.* Chicago: 1963.

Röpke, W., *German Commercial Policy.* London: 1934.

—— *The Social Crisis of our Time.* Chicago: 1950.

—— 'Will West Germany's free enterprise system survive?', in *The Commercial and Financial Chronicle.* New York: 14 June 1962.

Rosenberg, H., 'Political and social consequences of the Great Depression of 1873–1896 in Central Europe', in *EHR*: 1943.

——/Brady, R. A./Townsend, M. E., 'The Economic impact of Imperial Germany', in *JEH*: 1943.

Rostas, L., 'Industrial production, Productivity and Labor distribution in Britain, Germany and the US, 1935–7', in *Economic Journal*: 1943.

Roth, G., *Social Democrats in Imperial Germany.* Totowa: 1963.

Sanders, W. S., *Trade Unionism in Germany.* London: 1916.

Schacht, H., *My first 76 Years.* London: 1955.

Schmidt, C. T., *German Business Cycles, 1924–33.* New York: 1934.

Schmitz, C-J., 'German non-ferrous metal production in the early nineteenth century', in *JEEH*: 1972.

Schoenbaum, D., *Hitler's Social Revolution. Class and Status in Nazi Germany, 1933–39*.

Schweitzer, A., 'Big Business and the Nazi party in Germany', in *Journal of Business*: 1946.

—— 'Schacht's regulation of money and capital markets', in *Journal of Finance*: 1948.

—— 'Business power in the Nazi regime', in *Zeitschrift für Nationalökonomie*: 1960.

—— *Big Business in the Third Reich*. Indiana: 1964.

Seidel, R., *The Trade Union Movement of Germany*. Amsterdam: 1928.

Sering, M., *Germany under the Dawes Plan*. London: 1929.

Shanahan, W. O., *German Protestants face the Social Question*. Indiana: 1954.

Sheehan, J. J., 'Conflict and cohesion among German élites in the nineteenth century', in *MESH*.

Shorter, E., *Social Change and Social Policy in Bavaria, 1800–1860*. Harvard Dissertation; 1968.

—— 'Sexual change and illegitimacy: the European experience', in *MESH*.

Siemens, G., *History of the House of Siemens*. Two vols., Freiburg: 1957.

Simon, W. H., *The Failure of the Prussian Reform Movement*. Cambridge: 1955.

Simpson, A. E., 'The struggle for control of the German economy', in *JMH*: 1959.

Skalweit, A. K. F., *The German War Food Policy*. New Haven: 1927.

Stearns, P., 'Adaptation to Industrialization: German workers as a test case', in *Central European History*: 1970.

Stolper, G., *German Realities*. New York: 1948.

——/Häuser, K./Borchardt, K., *The German Economy, 1870 to the Present*. London: 1967.

Stolper, W. F., 'The labor force and industrial development in Soviet Germany', in *QJE*: 1957.

—— *The Structure of the East German Economy*. Harvard: 1960.

Strain, J., *Feminism and Political Radicalism in the German Social Democratic Movement, 1890–1914*. University of California Dissertation: 1964.

Sweezy, M., 'Distribution of Wealth and income under the Nazis', *Review of Economic Statistics*: 1939.

Bibliography

—— *The Structure of the Nazi Economy*. Cambridge: 1941.
—— 'German corporate profits, 1926–38', in *QJE*: 1940.

Temin, P., 'The beginning of the Depression in Germany', in *EHR*: 1971.
Tilly, R., *Financial Institutions and Industrialization in the Rhineland*. Wisconsin: 1966.
—— 'The political economy of public finance and the industrialization of Prussia, 1815–66', in *JEH*: 1966.
—— ' "Soll und Haben": recent German economic history and the problem of economic development', in *JEH*: 1969.
Tipton, F. B., 'Farm labor and power politics in Germany, 1850–1914', in *JEH*: 1974.
Tirrell, S. R., *German Agrarian Politics after Bismarck's Fall*. New York: 1951.
Townsend, M. E., *The Rise and Fall of Germany's Colonial Empire, 1884–1918*. New York: 1930.
Turner, H. A., 'Big business and the rise of Hitler', in *American Historical Review*: 1969.
—— 'The Ruhrlade. Secret cabinet of heavy industry in the Weimar republic', in *Central European History*: 1970.

Veblen, T., *Imperial Germany and the Industrial Revolution*: 1939.
Vogl, F., *German Business after the Economic Miracle*. London: 1973.
Voight, F., 'German experience with Cartels and their control during pre-war and post-war periods', in J. P. Miller (Ed.), *Competition, Cartels and their Regulation*. Amsterdam: 1962.

Walker, M., *Germany and the Emigration, 1816–85*. Harvard: 1964.
—— 'Home towns and state administration. South German Politics, 1815–30', in *Political Science*: 1967.
—— 'Napoleonic Germany and the Hometown communities', in *Central European History*: 1969.
—— *German Home Towns: Community, State and General Estate, 1648–1871*. Ithaca: 1971.
Waltershausen, A. S. v., *The History of the German Economy, 1815–1914*. Jena: 1920.
Wallich, H. C., *Mainsprings of the German Revival*. New Haven: 1955.
Wander, H., 'Migration and the German economy', in

B. Thomas (Ed.), *Economics of International Migration*: 1958.

Wemelsfelder, J., 'The short-term effect of the lowering of import duties in Germany', in *Economic Journal*: 1960.

Wendel, H. C. M., *The Evolution of Industrial Freedom in Prussia, 1845–9*. New York: 1921.

Wolfe, M., 'The development of Nazi monetary policy', in *JEH*, 1955.

Wunderlich, F., 'Germany's defense economy and the decay of capitalism', in *QJE*: 1938.

—— *German Labor Courts*. Chapel Hill: 1946.

—— 'The National Socialist agrarian program', in *Social Research*: 1946.

—— *Farm Labor in Germany, 1810–1945*. Princeton, 1961.

Index

Administration, 15; reforms of
Vormärz, 18–19, 20, 27, 37;
weakened during 1848, 35;
under Bismarck, 56, 70, 80,
81; bureaucracy during World
War I, 99; under Weimar
Republic, 104, 113, 114;
during 3rd Reich, 115
Agricultural Revolution:
eighteenth century
innovations, 17: farm
consolidation, 21, new ideas,
30, 138, 139–40, 140–1;
results of, 22–3, 35–6.
Agriculture: predominance in
1800, 2; poverty in rural areas,
6, 17; results of agricultural
revolution, 22–3, 35–6; growth
cycles, 46, 62; crisis of 1857,
47; in 1870s, 67–8; allied with
industry, 71; declining
economic significance, 72, 73,
76, 91; agricultural tariffs,
79–80, 84, 85; need for
self-sufficiency in World War
I, 97; state control, 98; under
Weimar Republic, 111; during
3rd Reich, 116, 120; socialist
land reform in DDR, 125–6;

agriculture in BRD, 128. See
also Agricultural Revolution;
Landowning Aristocracy
Air Force, 124
Allied Powers: unanimity
during World War II, 122,
123; political tensions after,
125, 129
Alsace, 66, 106
America. See United States of
America
Anti-semitism, 86, 119
Aristocracy. See Landowning
Aristocracy
Armaments Industry, 3, 7, 98,
120, 121, 123–4
Army: in 1800, 1, 15; in 1848,
34; Bismarck's military
policies, 56, 59, 80; opposes
Caprivi, 85; Wehrverein, 95;
military strength in 1914, 95,
97; during World War I, 98,
100; supports Weimar
Republic, 103, 104; under 3rd
Reich, 113, 117, 118, 119, 121,
122; post-war, 131
Association of German Iron and
Steel Industrialists, 66
Austria, 33, 38, 51; economic

Index

Austria—*contd.*
conflict with Prussia, 48–9, 70; in World War II, 121

Banks, 4, 24, 29; first banks founded, 31, 36; relations with industry, 39, 40, 47–8, 53, 64–5, 74–5, 89; economic nationalism, 65–6; joint-stock banks predominate, 48, 52, 59, 64; reorganisation, 51, 53; Berlin banks, 59, 64–5, 90, 110; effects of foreign policy, 93; support free trade, 94; during World War I, 98, 99; finance inflation, 106; state intervention, 109; liquidity problems, 110, 112, 114; in 3rd Reich, 115, 120; in post-war BRD, 129

Bavaria, 25, 38, 49

Bebel, August, 57, 102

Belgium, 26, 39, 49, 51, 121; 'battle for the Ruhr', 107

Berlin, 3, 4, 38, 99; banking centre, 50–1, 59, 63, 64, 90, 110; population growth, 76, 87

Bethmann-Hollweg, Theobald von, 95

Beuth, P. C. W., 24; biography, 133

Bismarck, Otto von: unification of Germany, 49, 50; strengthens power of state, 55, 56, 70; reaction to tensions in state, 80, 81, 82–3; tariff policy, 66, 69, 90; resigns, 83; legacy, 84, 90, 92, 101

Black Market, 99, 130

Born, Stephan, 57; biography, 133–4

Borsig, A., 26, 135; biography 134

Bourgeoisie. *See* Middle Class

Brandenburg, 18

BRD *See* German Federal Republic

Brest-Litowsk Negotiations, 99

Brüning, Heinrich, 112

Bucharest Negotiations, 99

Building trade, 65, 90, 117

Bülow, Prince Bernhard von, 94

Bunsen, R. W. von, 42; biography, 134

Bureaucracy. *See* Administration

Capital and Investment: shortage to 1848, 4, 8, 24, 38–9; capital accumulation, 31; foreign capital, 36, 37, 39, 42, 51; concentration, 51; growth in share capital, 59, 61; investment in 1880s, 74, 75; rise in savings, 87; shortage during inflation, 106, 107–8; foreign capital during Weimar Republic, 108, 110; capital concentration, 109, 110. *See also* Banks

Caprivi, Leo von, 79, 84–5, 90

Cartels. *See* Monopolistic Agreements

Central Association of German Industrialists, 69, 94, 95

Central European Customs Union, 38, 48

Central Union of German Industrialists, 85

Chemical Industry, 26; research and innovation, 42, 45, 134, 136, 139, 140; growth after 1860, 50, 73; large firms predominate, 75; in 1914, 88; under Weimar state, 108; cartels, 109; during World War II, 122; post-war controls, 124; in Soviet zone, 126

Church, 37, 69, 77, 137, 142

Cities: as markets and ports, 2; manufacturing centres, 3; foreign trading centres, 4; poverty in, 4, 17; reform of administration, 19, 31; growth, 74, 75, 76, 77; bombed in World War II, 122

162

Index

Index

Investment. *See* Capital and Investment

Iron Industry: to 1840, 25–6; rising demand, 36; liberalisation, 38; innovations, 135, 140; first amalgamations, 40, 41; growth in 1860s, 51, 62; influence of banks, 65; cartels, 74; growth to 1914, 88; shortage of iron ore, 106; in Soviet zone, 126; in BRD, 129, 132. *See also* Association of German Iron and Steel Industrialists

Joint-Stock Companies: Founded, 37, 38; neo-feudalism, 41; 1857 crisis, 47; repeal of registration duty, 53; importance in economy, 63

Judiciary, 19, 20

Junkers, 114. *See also* Landowning Aristocracy

Kekule, F. A., 42; biography, 136–7

Ketteler, W. E. von, 57; biography, 137

Kirchoff, G. R., 42; biography, 137

Kolping, Adolf, 57; biography, 137

Koppe, J. G., 30; biography, 138

Krupp, Alfred, 26, 40, 82; biography, 138

Kunth, G. J. C., 24, 25, 133; biography, 138–9

Landowning Aristocracy: in 1800, 1, 15, 17; farm consolidation, 20–1; conservatism, 27; influence in Vormärz, 29; in 1848, 33; ally with industry and banking to preserve power, 34, 35, 42–3, 44, 54, 70, 71; under

Bismarck, 51–2; protectionist views, 68, 70, 78–9, 85; alliance breaks, 77, 78, 83, 95; decline in political and economic power after 1900, 95; in Weimar state, 103, 104, 106, 113, 114; during 3rd Reich, 116; dispossessed in Soviet zone, 125–6. *See also* Union of Farmers

Lasalle, Ferdinand, 57, 137

Legislation: reorganisation of legal system, 19; trade laws during Vormärz, 23; Delbrück's laws, 52–3; Bismarck's social legislation, 81, 84, 93; trade union and worker laws under Weimar state, 105

Liberals: in 1848, weakened by fear of social revolution, 33, 34, 35; Bismarck combines liberal and conservative claims, 54, 55; divisions among liberals, 55; want political responsibility and democracy, 56, 69; discredited, 63, 70; abandon Bismarck, 83; oppose Caprivi, 85; political and economic crisis defeats liberalism 1929, 113. *See also* Parliamentary Movement

Liebig, Justus von, 30, 42; biography, 139

Lorraine, 66, 89

Ludendorff, Eric von, 99

Ludwig II, King of Bavaria, 49

Machine Construction Industry, 59, 74, 90, 108, 124, 135–136

Marshall Plan, 130

Marx, K., 8, 57, 141

Mayer, J. 26; biography, 139

Mefo Bills, 118, 119, 120

Mercantilism. *See* State Intervention

Index

Index